Decks
& Decking

Weekend DIY

Decks & Decking

15 step-by-step projects

Quick and easy ideas to enhance your garden

Alan & Gill Bridgewater

NEW HOLLAND

Reprinted in 2007
First published in 2002 by New Holland Publishers (UK) Ltd
London · Cape Town · Sydney · Auckland

Garfield House, 86–88 Edgware Road, London W2 2EA, United Kingdom
www.newhollandpublishers.com

80 McKenzie Street, Cape Town 8001, South Africa

Unit 1, 66 Gibbes Street, Chatswood, NSW 2067, Australia

218 Lake Road, Northcote, Auckland, New Zealand

ISBN: 978 1 84330 142 4

3 5 7 9 10 8 6 4 2

Editorial Direction: Rosemary Wilkinson
Project Editor: Clare Johnson
Production: Hazel Kirkman

Designed and created for New Holland by AG&G BOOKS
Project design: AG&G Books   Project construction: AG&G Books and John Heming
Planting and props: AG&G Books and Vana Haggerty
Photography: AG&G Books and Ian Parsons   Illustrator: Gill Bridgewater
Editor: Fiona Corbridge   Designer: Glyn Bridgewater

Reproduction by Pica Digital Pte Ltd, Singapore
Printed and bound in Malaysia by Times Offset (M) Sdn. Bhd.

Conversion chart

To convert the metric measurements given in this book to imperial measurements, simply multiply the figure given in the text by the relevant number shown in the table alongside. Bear in mind that conversions will not necessarily work out exactly, and you will need to round the figure up or down slightly. (Do not use a combination of metric and imperial measurements – for accuracy, keep to one system.)

To convert	Multiply by
millimetres to inches	0.0394
metres to feet	3.28
metres to yards	1.093
sq millimetres to sq inches	0.00155
sq metres to sq feet	10.76
sq metres to sq yards	1.195
cu metres to cu feet	35.31
cu metres to cu yards	1.308
grams to pounds	0.0022
kilograms to pounds	2.2046
litres to gallons	0.22

Contents

Traditional
boardwalk
26

Decking
steps
30

Japanese
engawa
34

Circular
patio
38

Country
walk path
42

Japanese
bridge
46

Planter
tubs
50

Chequerboard
decking patio
54

Garden decking
with steps
58

Bench seat
and safety rail
62

Tree
ring seat
66

Adirondack
chair
70

Patio with
sandpit
76

Hillside
decking
82

Waterside
raised decking
88

Introduction

My brother's pied-à-terre in a Cornish seaside village is an exciting homage to wood – the walls are made from riven oak, the roof is covered in wood, the front door is made from wood salvaged from a boatyard, and the stairs are made from walnut. But most impressively of all, the whole place is a wonderland of wooden decking. There is a small suspension bridge walkway from the gate to the first level, and raised decking jutting out from the house. The house backs on to the sea, and decking terraces lead down the cliff face to the beach, where a beautiful decking pier runs out to the sea. And so the idea for this book took off...

A brief history

There is some evidence that wooden walkways and platforms were built in ancient times, however decking as we know it today had its beginnings in countries such as Czechoslovakia, Germany, Poland and Norway, and later in the pioneer towns of America, Australia and South Africa. In village and pioneer societies where wood was abundant and time was short, the best way to construct paths, walkways, porches and platforms was to build them from rough-sawn timber.

A beautiful covered porch in Rosedown, USA, complete with wooden baluster pillars, window shutters and rocking chairs. Note the use of mixed-width decking boards.

Be inspired

The exciting thing about building decking is its immediacy. It might well be necessary to mix a small amount of concrete for the footings, but apart from that you can simply float the decking over an existing garden with all its problems (such as an old concrete patio that you just haven't got the energy to get rid of, a rocky outcrop that simply cannot be moved, or a patch of scrub). If you want to give your garden a swift makeover, take advantage of a splendid view, or simply expand your living space, this is the book for you.

Best of luck

The perfect place to spend a long, lazy afternoon – a stunning decking patio by a pool. The rugged, rough-sawn boards and the found posts look good in this setting.

Health and safety

Many woodworking procedures are potentially dangerous, so before starting work on the projects, check through the following list:

- ✔ Make sure that you are fit and strong enough for the task ahead of you. If you have doubts, ask your doctor for specific advice.

- ✔ Always use a safety electricity circuit breaker between the power socket and mains power tools. Never use a mains power tool if the lawn is wet.

- ✔ If possible, use battery-powered tools rather than those with cables, because they are safer for these types of outdoor project.

- ✔ When you are lifting large weights from ground level, such as main posts and beams, minimize the risk of back strain by bending your knees, hugging the item close to your body, and keeping the spine upright.

- ✔ If items look too heavy to lift on your own, ask others to help. Don't risk injury.

- ✔ Wear a dust-mask and goggles when using a power tool such as a jigsaw, and when sanding pressure-treated wood, because it is impregnated with toxic preservative.

- ✔ Never operate a machine such as a power drill, or attempt a difficult lifting or manoeuvring task, if you are overtired or using medication.

- ✔ Keep a first-aid kit and telephone within easy reach.

- ✔ Allow children to watch at a safe distance and help with small tasks, but never leave them unsupervised.

Part 1
Techniques

Designing and planning

Decking is fun to build, but only if you spend time carefully designing and planning all the details of the project. It is vital to study the site, ask other family members for their views, consult neighbours if the intended construction could conceivably affect them, draw up plans and list materials, before you start ordering wood. This section explains what you need to know.

Looking at your outdoor space

Assessing your garden

Walk around the garden and consider your requirements for the decking. How do you want to use it? Will it be an area for sunbathing or for sitting in the shade? Do you want it for evening barbecues, or for the children to play on? Do you want the decking to be physically linked to the house, or set in isolation? Look at the levels of the land, note the position of the sun at different times of day and the prevailing direction of the wind, and observe the way the family usually moves around the garden. Think about possible sites.

Style considerations

Take into account the style of your house and its setting. You may decide that the decking should continue the theme of the house, and look folksy or modern, for example. Alternatively, the decking could be a separate statement, providing a contrast to the style of the interior decor.

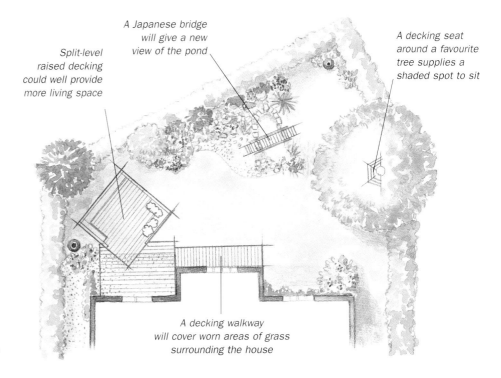

Split-level raised decking could well provide more living space

A Japanese bridge will give a new view of the pond

A decking seat around a favourite tree supplies a shaded spot to sit

A decking walkway will cover worn areas of grass surrounding the house

Whatever the size of your garden, there is a good chance that there is room for a decking feature – perhaps a patio or a decking bridge. Draw up a plan of your garden and consider the possibilities, using several copies to sketch in various options.

Design

Shape, form and structure

Once you have a clear idea of what you want to build, its site and overall style, you need to work out the design in more detail. What shape do you want it to be? Do you want the decking to be raised up high with feature stairs and decorative railings? Do the posts need to be set in concrete for stability? Does the decking have to wrap around the corner of the house, as for a Japanese engawa? Is the form so structurally complex that it will require lots of bolts and braces? Will the decking incorporate existing features such as trees and rocky outcrops?

Form and function

It is fine to allow form to dominate the design for a proposed project when it is no more than a plant tub or small patio, but for other projects, safety reasons dictate that function must be the main consideration. For example, when you are building raised decking with steps and railings, or a chair that has to bear your weight and also fold up for storage, function is much more important than form. The item has to be structurally sound and safe to use before pattern, texture and colour come into the picture.

Wood types

Always use the best wood that you can afford, especially when building more complex, time-consuming projects such as a large area of decking. If money is no object, select long-lasting woods such as redwood or oak. If you need to keep costs to a minimum, use pressure-treated pine. Either way, make sure that the wood is free from splits, twists, soft waney edges, decay, dead knots and insect infestation.

Drawing your designs

Phone three suppliers and ask about sizes and prices. Let's say, for example, that you need two 1.25 m lengths of wood. The cheapest option might be for you to order a single 3 m length and cut the wood to size yourself, rather than ordering two 1.25 m lengths. If this is the case, there will be some wastage, therefore would it be better to enlarge the project so that you use two 1.5 m lengths?

Once you have made all the decisions regarding length and cost, sketch the design on paper – the plan view, front and side views, and the details. Draw in

the overall dimensions, the dimensions of the various sections, the number of pieces of wood, and any details concerning joints and fixings. Make a list of the component parts – the number of lengths of each type of wood, and the number of bolts and fixings required.

Before diving headlong into ordering wood and building, sit down in the garden with a piece of paper, inspirational pictures collected from magazines, and samples of decking materials. Spend some time considering the options. Design the project so that it suits all your needs.

Planning

First steps

Once you have ordered the wood, plan out the logistics of the project, from the moment the wood arrives through to the actual order of work. Decide where you are going to stack the wood and whether you will need to buy more tools or sharpen old ones. If concrete is required, establish whether you need to hire a cement mixer. If you are planning to work on a Sunday, find out if there is a nearby shop where you can replenish supplies if, for example, you run out of screws. Is it feasible to complete the project in a single weekend, or would it be better to spread the work over two weekends? Will you have to wait for concrete to cure, or can you plan the tasks so that the concrete dries out overnight?

Permission and safety

Check that there are no planning restrictions governing the type of structure you intend to build. Depending upon where you live, you might need permission before you can erect a "permanent structure", although the definition of this can vary. Some planning departments only define decking as permanent if it has a full concrete foundation slab; others make decisions based on height off the ground and number of steps.

Follow proper safety procedures and wear gloves to guard your hands against splinters and abrasion, goggles to protect your eyes, and strong boots to stop your feet being crushed. Wear a dust-mask if sanding pressure-treated wood or wood that has been brushed with preservative.

Planning checklist

- ✔ Are there any sawmills in your area? These will be the most economical source of materials.

- ✔ Can you save money by modifying the projects to suit a particular size or type of wood?

- ✔ Are local suppliers willing to deliver small quantities of wood?

- ✔ Is there adequate access to your garden, with a wide gateway and possibly room for a lorry to turn?

- ✔ If the wood is unloaded in your drive, or at your gate, will it cause problems or pose a danger?

- ✔ How are you going to move the wood from the drive to the site? Will you need help from friends?

Materials

The only reliable way to get top-quality wood is to go to the timberyard and choose it yourself, rather than ordering it unseen. Phone around for the best quotes first, then arm yourself with a detailed list of your needs – type of wood, quantity, and the various lengths and sections – and go to look at the wood on offer. Choose the boards yourself, one by one. The following section shows you how.

Using timber and other decking materials

Width, thickness and length

Timberyards sell wood that is termed "nominal rough-sawn" and "surfaced smooth". Sawn wood comes in exactly the sizes described, so a piece of 60 mm-wide rough-sawn wood is actually that size. However, a piece of 60 mm-wide surfaced-smooth wood measures something less. Wood is sold as standard sections, such as square, rectilinear or round, and comes in 2-, 3- and 4-metre lengths. Generally, you get a better deal if you buy long lengths and cut to fit.

Timber types and textures

Some timberyards offer various top-quality wood species such as redwood, cedar and oak, which are long-lasting and resistant to rot and insect attack. More commonly, timberyards tend to sell pine that has been pressure-treated with either brown or green chemical preservatives.

We favour using rough-sawn wood for the projects, which we swiftly sand to remove splinters, and then protect and colour with washes of garden paint, or with a traditional wash made from a mixture of lime and water.

Other materials

Woven plastic sheeting, gravel and shingle, ballast, sand and cement, and all manner of screws, nails and bolts are used in the projects. Gravel and shingle are used as decorative spreads and as a hardcore, and ballast (a mixture of sand and gravel) is used when making concrete. When selecting nails, screws and bolts, opt for plated or galvanized types. We generally prefer to use screws rather than nails, because they have more holding power. Bolts are good when you need an extra-strong joint, such as when fitting joists to posts, or building frames.

Buying wood

If you can get access to a flatbed truck for your visit to the timberyard, you can take the wood away with you, rather than waiting for it to be delivered. Take a tape measure and hand-pick every board, batten and post on your list. Don't be intimidated. Reject wood that is split, twisted or in any way less than perfect.

Caution
Pressure-treated timber
Wear gloves when handling newly treated wood, and avoid contact with the sawdust. Wash your hands before eating or drinking.

*Opposite page: A selection of materials suitable for making the projects in this book. **1** Gravel, **2** Plastic sheeting, **3** "Fence capping", **4** Preserved decking, **5** Pressure-treated decking, **6** Grooved decking, **7** Wide decking board, **8** Standard screws, **9** Decking screws, **10** Untreated decking, **11** Acorn finial, **12** Standard nails, **13** Coach bolt, **14** Joist, **15** Post, **16** Round-section post, **17** Wood chips.*

Concrete and other post fixing-materials

Most decking has to be set on some sort of foundation.

- ✔ For a small area of low-level decking: dig post holes, set posts on 100 mm of hardcore, fill up holes with gravel.

- ✔ For decking on solid ground: place pre-cast concrete pads on the ground, set the posts directly in position.

- ✔ For damp, compacted soil: dig post holes, add 100 mm of hardcore, insert posts, fill up with dryish concrete mix.

- ✔ For sandy soil: dig holes, line with plywood, add 100 mm of hardcore, insert posts, fill up with stiff concrete mix.

- ✔ For sandy soil, with the footing extended above ground level: dig post holes, set a fibre tube or former in the holes so that the top is at the desired level, put 100 mm of gravel into the former and top it up with concrete, and push the anchor-fixing into the wet concrete.

Caution

Cement and lime are both corrosive. Always wear a dust-mask, gloves and goggles. If you get the powder on your skin, especially if your skin is damp, wash it off immediately with copious amounts of water.

Tools

Tools are one of the main keys to successful woodwork. A few carefully chosen, medium-priced tools will make every task a pleasure to complete. But to save on costs, avoid splashing out on a complete new set of tools, and just start out by using the tools that you already have to hand. Buy new tools when you really need to. Here is a list of tools which, in an ideal world, would reside in your toolkit.

Useful tools for building decking

Tools for preparing the site

You need a large fibreglass tape measure for measuring the site, wooden pegs and string for setting out the limits of the decking, and a club hammer for banging in pegs. You also require a spade for cutting away turf and digging holes, and a bucket, wheelbarrow, shovel and rake for all the earth-moving tasks. Choose tools to suit your strength and height – for example, you can buy different sizes of spade and sledgehammer. A spirit level is neccessary for checking levels, both on the decking and when setting out pegs.

Measuring and marking

A small tape measure is used for measuring lengths and widths, a square for drawing and checking right angles, and a compass or a pair of dividers for drawing circle-based curves.

A clutch of good, strong carpenter's pencils is vital – they last longer than ordinary pencils, and don't roll off the workbench. If you are making decking with angles greater or smaller than 90°, you also need either a bevel gauge or an engineer's protractor square.

Sawing wood

A couple of hand saws are always useful. We use a crosscut saw for cutting wood to length across the grain, and a rip saw for cutting a board down its length.

When it comes to cutting curves, we use an electric jigsaw. Occasionally, we use a hand coping saw for cutting tight curves and little details. If you particularly enjoy using power tools, consider obtaining a small combination mitre saw, which is a really good tool for making a large number of identical cuts.

Drilling and screwing

We use a straightforward electric drill for drilling deep, large-diameter holes, and a cordless drill in conjunction with a cross-point screwdriver bit for driving in screws. However, if the weather is damp, or we are too lazy to unroll the cable for the electric drill, we might use the cordless drill both for drilling holes and driving in screws. If, by the end of the day, the cordless drill has run out of power, we might also use the electric drill to drive in screws. If you intend to build a lot of decking, it's a good idea to invest in two cordless drills, so that you can always have one charging up in readiness.

Nailing

Before nailing, you need one of the drills to drill pilot holes, and then a claw hammer to knock in the nails. If the workpiece needs to be supported, to stop it shaking or bouncing, hold a sledgehammer or a club hammer at the back of it. We generally have at least two or three claw hammers on site, so that there is always one near to hand – on the ground, on the decking, somewhere on the woodpile, or on the workbench.

Holding and securing

Ideally, you need two portable workbenches so that you can cut long lengths of wood comfortably, without asking for help. We use two very cheap benches, and don't worry about giving them a lot of heavy treatment. If you are trying to cut costs, you could even work on a couple of old teachests. If you are doing most of the work on your own, you will also need a couple of large-size clamps for holding the workpiece in place while you are drilling holes and screwing. It is important to keep your back straight while you work, to avoid strain.

Tool hire

If your main interest is in the end results of a particular project, rather than in taking up woodwork and decking construction as a future hobby, it might be best to borrow the larger and more expensive tools. If you need a large sander or a cement mixer, the most sensible course of action is to hire the piece of equipment.

Caution
Power tools

Electricity, early-morning dew, buckets of water and wet hands are a potentially dangerous combination. If you do decide to use an electric drill instead of a portable drill, or an electric cement mixer, make sure that you use it in conjunction with an electricity circuit breaker.

A basic tool kit

For making the projects in this book, you will need to buy or borrow the tools shown below. All these basic, everyday tools can be bought from a general DIY store. Larger pieces of equipment can be hired from specialist hire shops.

Items that are not illustrated include a portable workbench, wheelbarrow and bucket (the last two are for making concrete, which may be necessary for fixing posts in the ground to support areas of decking).

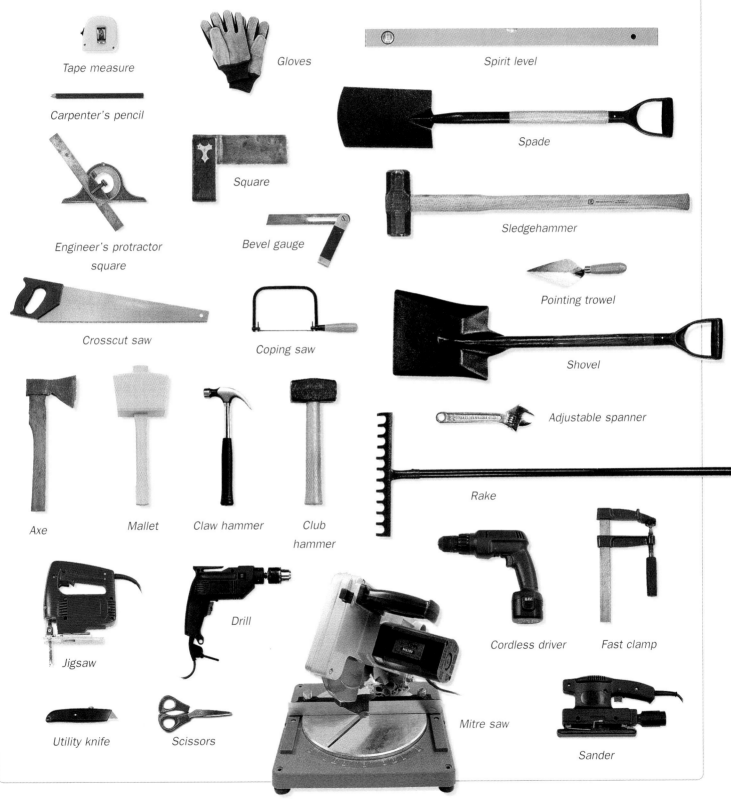

Tape measure

Gloves

Spirit level

Carpenter's pencil

Engineer's protractor square

Square

Bevel gauge

Spade

Sledgehammer

Pointing trowel

Crosscut saw

Coping saw

Shovel

Axe

Mallet

Claw hammer

Club hammer

Adjustable spanner

Rake

Jigsaw

Drill

Cordless driver

Fast clamp

Utility knife

Scissors

Mitre saw

Sander

Basic techniques

Once you have a clear understanding of the basic techniques, and you can handle the tools with confidence, building decking is an enjoyable experience. The secret is to work at an easy, comfortable pace, and not to rush things. Make sure you spend plenty of time assessing the intended site to ensure that it is suitable, measure accurately, and always double-check before you make a cut.

Marking out

Fixing the position of the posts

Once you have decided where you want to build the decking, establish the positions of the levels of decking and all the holes for the supporting posts. Fix a reference post in position and at the correct height, and then use pegs, string and the crossed diagonal method to relate all the other posts and levels to this point. We usually set the reference post on the high point of the site. The crossed diagonal method involves measuring each of the diagonals of a given rectangle (such as a marked-out site, or an area of decking), and ensuring that they are the same. If not, adjustments are made until they are.

Check that the diagonal measurements of the rectangle are identical

Check that the lengths of the rectangle's sides are equal

Due to the large scale of decking projects, it is often difficult to tell by eye alone if a rectangular structure – such as a decking framework – is square (has 90° corners). You need to use a tape measure to check the length, width and diagonal measurements.

Initial tasks

Preparing the site

Once you have worked out the precise position of the post holes, you need to make a decision about the existing foliage (lawn and plants) that is growing on the area that will be covered by the decking.

There is no problem if the decking is going to be high enough off the ground to walk under, but if it will be at a low level, remove the turf, roughly level the ground and lay a sheet of woven plastic over it, and then cover the plastic with gravel. This system not only controls the weeds, but also allows rainwater to drain away freely. If the decking is going to be positioned just clear of the ground, all you need do is level out the bumps, lay

down a piece of woven plastic sheet and then simply rest the decking directly on short piles or concrete pads, so the joists are not in contact with the earth.

Setting posts in the ground

Dig a hole down to firm ground, or to the depth required by local planning regulations. It needs to be twice as big as the post. Shovel about 100 mm of hardcore in the hole, and set the post in position. Pour in concrete to surround the post, filling up the hole to ground level. Tamp the concrete with a beam to release air bubbles, check that the post is upright with a spirit level, and then fix it in place with temporary battens.

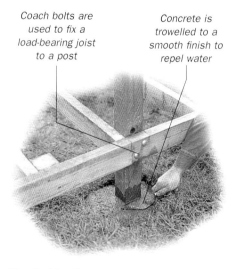

Coach bolts are used to fix a load-bearing joist to a post

Concrete is trowelled to a smooth finish to repel water

The decking framework (the main posts and joists) must be square, level and well secured. Concrete is used to fix the posts into the ground, so they do not move.

Cutting timber to size

Use an inexpensive, portable workbench to hold and support the workpiece. If you wish, use a clamp to grasp the wood firmly.

Cutting across the grain

A power saw is one option for cutting across the grain, but if you are a beginner it is best to use a new crosscut saw. Mark the line of cut with the square and pencil, and support the workpiece on the workbench. Place the saw to the waste side of the mark, draw the blade towards you to start the cut, and then continue sawing. When the saw is three-parts through the wood, hook your free hand round to support the waste, and complete the cut. A compound mitre saw is very useful when you need to repeat a large number of angled cuts, such as for laying decking at an angle to the frame.

Cutting curves

An electric jigsaw is a great tool for making curved cuts in wood up to about 50 mm thick. To use it, set the blade on the mark, switch on the power, and slowly advance to the waste side of the drawn line. To avoid dangerous kickbacks, always switch off the power before you draw the tool back from the workpiece.

Joints

Jointing with screws

There are various decking clips, fasteners and brackets on the market, but they are not the strongest, most attractive, or even the swiftest option. Also, many beginners find these fixings both expensive and confusing. For these reasons, we have opted for traditional joints held together either with cross-headed screws or with coach bolts. Occasionally, we use nails, but screws have more holding power and can be driven home or removed without damaging the wood. The order of work is to first drill a pilot hole, set the screw in place, and then drive it home with the cordless drill fitted with a cross-point screwdriver bit. If you are working with a partner, with one of you drilling the holes and the other driving in the screws, this technique can be just as fast as nailing.

Jointing with bolts

When an extra-strong joint is required, such as for fixing main joists to main posts, it is best to use a bolt. You can use a machine bolt with a washer at each end, or a coach bolt with a domed head and a square shoulder between the head and the shank. We prefer coach bolts, not only because the round head is more attractive, but they can also be fitted using a single spanner.

A cordless driver is the best tool for putting in screws

When you are laying boards on a large structure, always stagger the joints because this gives the best effect visually.

Washers are always used with coach-bolted joints, and a socket spanner or adjustable spanner to tighten up the nuts.

Finishing

Finishing

From the moment that your decking is completed, it will be subject to attack by the sun, rain and insects, so the wood needs to be protected. Traditionally, decking was limewashed or even tarred. There are many finishes on the market, from oils and resins to preservatives and varnishes. We generally prefer to start off with pressure-treated wood, and finish it with a colourwash. So we might mix lime with water, or thin down exterior-grade masonry paint until we have a wash. The resulting surface looks weathered, and instantly blends in with the garden.

Paths and patios

Wooden decking paths and patios look delightful and provide dry, level areas for safe and comfortable walking. They also attract your attention – the moment you see Japanese engawa decking running out of sight around the corner of a house, or a decking patio complete with a chair, you will be drawn to go and have a closer look. So for a striking, practical addition to your garden, opt for decking.

Constructing paths

Designing and planning

Walk around your garden and decide precisely where you want the path to be sited. Take note of the levels of the land, because these will have to be accommodated, and consider how the path will impact on your use of the garden.

Decide on the details of the decking's structure – the height off the ground and the position of the main beams – and use a tape measure, pegs and string to map out the site accordingly.

Building

Remove all large plants, level the ground, and dig out roots and large stones. Spread a layer of woven plastic weed-stop sheeting over the entire site and cover it with a generous layer of gravel. The wetter the site, the deeper the gravel needs to be, to ensure stability. Position the pressure-treated beams on the gravel and screw the decking boards in place.

A simple path that turns into a bridge complements the restrained planting scheme of this garden. The decking is supported on a concrete base and edged with log roll. The concrete supports for the three-board bridge are concealed behind the stacked slate walls.

INSPIRATIONS

A gently curving decking path, edged with cobbles, looks beautiful alongside a pond.

Decking boards lend themselves to crisp, geometrical layouts.

A path and water-crossing built from treated wood make an attractive feature.

Constructing a patio

Designing and planning

Think about how your garden looks over all the seasons, and then, in the light of your observations about sunshine, shade, being overlooked by neighbours, and so on, decide on the best place for siting the patio. Use a tape measure, pegs and string to mark out the boundaries of the site.

Building

If your garden is reasonably dry and level, and you want the patio close to the ground rather than raised up, you can use the same techniques as for building paths, and set the patio on a bed of plastic sheeting and gravel. Decking paths tend to consist of two tracks that run in straight or slightly curved lines, with decking boards bridging the tracks, but a patio offers you the opportunity to build a form that is both shapely and patterned. Once the plastic and gravel are in place, mark out the outer profile of the decking and divide it up with a pattern of joists set 300–450 mm apart at their centres. Make sure that the pattern of joists relates to the planned layout or pattern of your decking, so that there is plenty of support for the ends of the boards.

This patio and path uses a mix of straight boards and wedge-shaped segments. The decking is laid on gravel and set at the same depth as the lawn for easy mowing.

This generously sized ground-level decking looks ideally suited to the country house setting (New Orleans, USA). The owners needed a large seating area for barbecues and family gatherings. They wanted the patio to complement the existing tree, which offers some shade. The key to this type of decking patio is establishing a firm, level base (a low-lying framework).

A simple layout of decking tiles is perfectly suited to a small yard or balcony garden.

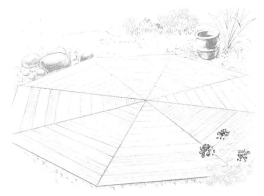

An octagonal patio is attention-grabbing. It is also easier to build than a circular patio.

A path linking the house to the garden. Well-trodden routes are prime sites for decking.

Decking

Decking can invigorate a family's use of their outdoor space, allowing many more activities to take place there. The space can be transformed by an area of raised decking standing high above the garden, or a subtle Japanese engawa running around the house, or even an island decking. Decking is also a crafty way of making a difficult-to-use area, such as a bank, participate fully in the life of the garden.

Constructing an engawa

Designing and planning
In a traditional Japanese garden, an *engawa* is a strip of low-level wooden decking that encircles the house, linking it to the garden. If you like the idea of having your own, walk around your house and have a good look at the levels of the land. Is it possible for an engawa to have a free passage around the house, or will it have to bridge immovable obstacles such as drainpipes? If you have to bridge drains, make sure that your decking includes inspection hatches. If there are existing paths, steps and trees, you will have to decide whether to leave them in place and run the decking over or around them, or whether to remove them. Use a tape measure, pegs and string to mark out the route of the engawa.

Building
Mark out the position of the footings at no more than 2 m apart, dig holes, and concrete short stub posts into place. Cover the site with plastic, topped off with gravel. Bridge the posts with beams and link the beams with joists. Bridge the beams with decking boards.

A Japanese teahouse with an engawa walkway in southern California, USA. The timber decking is minimal and practical, echoing the design of the building.

INSPIRATIONS

Stepped decking with an integral bench and railing, and under-seat storage space.

Low-level decking is ideal for a pond-side patio. A tree has been incorporated for shade.

Raised decking with steps and a handrail. The trellis screens off the neighbouring garden.

Island decking

Island decking can be built just about anywhere in the garden, so you can site it to take advantage of views, evening sunshine, afternoon shade, or whatever you wish. Use a tape measure, pegs and string to mark out the location of the footings. Dig holes and concrete the posts in position. Screw the main beams to the posts, make adjustments to correct the levels, and bolt the beams in place. Trim the tops off the posts, set joists on the beams and lay the decking as already described.

A simple island decking with an integral bench seat. The wood has been limewashed to create a cool, weathered effect (a welcome change to the popular red-brown finishes).

Raised decking with steps

Raised decking with steps is a great option for a home that is several steps above ground level, where there is a need to build decking that is close to the house but not actually attached to it.

Use a tape measure, pegs and string to establish the position of the footings and to mark out the total plan area. Concrete the posts into the ground. The secret of building decking of this type is to start by bolting a registration or ledger beam as close as possible to the house, and then use it as a marker for all the other levels.

Raised decking with steps in New Orleans, USA. The owners had to deal with the problem of varying ground levels in their garden, so the ideal solution was to lay decking to cover the entire area.

A decking porch with steps and railing provides an area for walking and sitting.

A porch walkway with a handrail. Trellis is used to cover the gap underneath.

Traditional raised decking overlooking the sea makes a perfect area for relaxation.

Decking additions

Once the decking is in place, additions such as railings, steps and benches offer you an opportunity for artistic expression in terms of pattern and form. If you like Japanese lattice screens, Swiss cottage fretwork, bold modernism or American folk colours, now is the time to incorporate them into your design. For sources of inspiration, have a root through the interior decor and architecture sections in a bookshop or library.

Constructing steps

A multi-level decking incorporating bench seating in Louisiana, USA. Steps are an obvious requirement for sloping sites and can be the most challenging aspect of the whole job of design and construction. Broad steps are more people-friendly than narrow stairways.

Designing and planning

Look at the site and use a tape measure, batten and pencil to establish the total distance along the ground that the flight of steps will cover, and the total height from one level to another. Decide on the riser height (between 100 mm and 180 mm), divide the total height by this number, and minus one to give the number of risers. Divide the horizontal distance along the ground by the number of risers to obtain the maximum depth of the treads.

Building

For the stringers (sides of the steps), you have a choice between zigzag stringers or solid planks. Start by measuring and cutting the two stringers so that they run parallel to each other, with their feet on the ground and their heads firmly fixed to the edge of the decking. Once the two stringers are in place, the rest is easy. A simple box dais does not have stringers.

INSPIRATIONS

This delightfully simple bridge or walkway draws inspiration from Japanese gardens.

Built-in seating with railings and planters, following a symmetrical arrangement.

Two planters bridged with boards provide a simple seat. A backrest is optional.

Railings

Ask your local planning department for advice and information about railing height, the recommended distance apart for the main posts, and other safety factors. The primary concern is that children cannot get their heads stuck between rails, or slip between the decking and the bottom horizontal rail. Consider your particular needs. Do the railings need to be especially safe because the decking is high off the ground, or are they more of a privacy screen or a windbreak? The order of work is to bolt the main posts in place, top them with the banister rail, and then fit the baluster rails or screen. The balusters afford you the opportunity to build in decorative details.

Benches

Look at the seating in your house in order to decide on the height and depth for a bench (seats are likely to be about 400 mm above the ground). A bench can be fixed as part of the railings around the decking, or it can be freestanding so you have the option of moving it around. If a railing also forms the back of the bench, remember that children might climb on the bench, so the railing will need to be made higher. Once you have worked out the height of the seat, and the height and angle of the backrest, the actual building is very straightforward.

High railings combined with a lattice screen. The owners wanted to make sure that the raised decking was safe for their small children and pets to use.

A beautifully crafted bench makes this wonderful roofed decking even more enticing. Imagine sitting there and soaking up the view after a hard day's work.

A bench built around a tree is a great place to sit – perfect for escaping from the sun.

What better way of enjoying decking than to stretch out on a home-made sun lounger?

A traditional American Adirondack chair is just the thing for a decking porch.

Part 2
Projects

Traditional boardwalk

There is something very special about a traditional decking boardwalk – it looks spectacular in its simplicity, and feels good underfoot. The act of walking on the boards produces a characteristic drumming that will remind you of a seaside pier. This project is for the simplest kind of boardwalk – a straight path – but you could design one that turns corners, follows a curve or changes level.

★
Easy

Making time
One weekend
One day for putting the beams in place, and one day for fitting and fixing the decking

Considering the design

The traditional boardwalk is very simple in construction – just two lines of posts banged directly into the ground, with beams lapped on to the posts to make two parallel rails, which are topped with weathered, rough-sawn decking boards. The tops of the 100 mm-square posts stand about 150 mm clear of the ground, allowing the boardwalk to skim over uneven land. This walkway is quick and easy to build, and suitable for various situations, such as over a lawn, or through an area of wooded scrub.

Getting started

Study your site and decide on the route of the boardwalk. Look at the ground and make checks with the spirit level to establish how far above ground level the decking needs to be, if your requirements are different to the specifications of the project (170 mm above ground level).

Measure the length of the proposed boardwalk from one end to the other to calculate the wood required. We have quoted quantities per 2 m length of boardwalk. Order the wood and when it is delivered, stack it as close as possible to the site. Set out your workbenches and tools, and you are ready to begin.

Overall dimensions and general notes

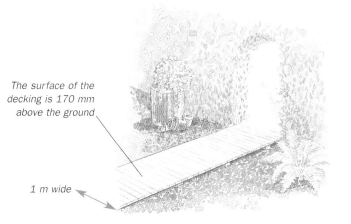

The surface of the decking is 170 mm above the ground

1 m wide

A traditional boardwalk will look good in just about any garden. It can be painted or left a natural colour.

You will need

Tools

✔ Two portable workbenches
✔ Pencil, ruler, tape measure and square
✔ Crosscut saw
✔ Wooden mallet
✔ Small hand axe
✔ Pegs and string
✔ Spade
✔ Sledgehammer
✔ Spirit level
✔ Cordless electric drill with a cross-point screwdriver bit
✔ Drill bit to match the size of the screws
✔ Two 5 mm-thick offcuts to use as spacers (either sawn wood or plywood)

Materials

(All rough-sawn pieces of pine include excess length for wastage. All the wood is pressure-treated with preservative.)

For approximately 2 m of boardwalk, 1 m wide

✔ Pine: 1 rough-sawn piece, 3 m long and 100 mm square section (posts)
✔ Pine: 2 rough-sawn pieces, 2 m long, 90 mm wide and 40 mm thick (beams)
✔ Pine: 10 rough-sawn pieces, 2 m long, 100 mm wide and 20 mm thick (decking boards)
✔ Zinc-plated, countersunk cross-headed screws: 100 x 90 mm no. 10

Exploded view of the traditional boardwalk

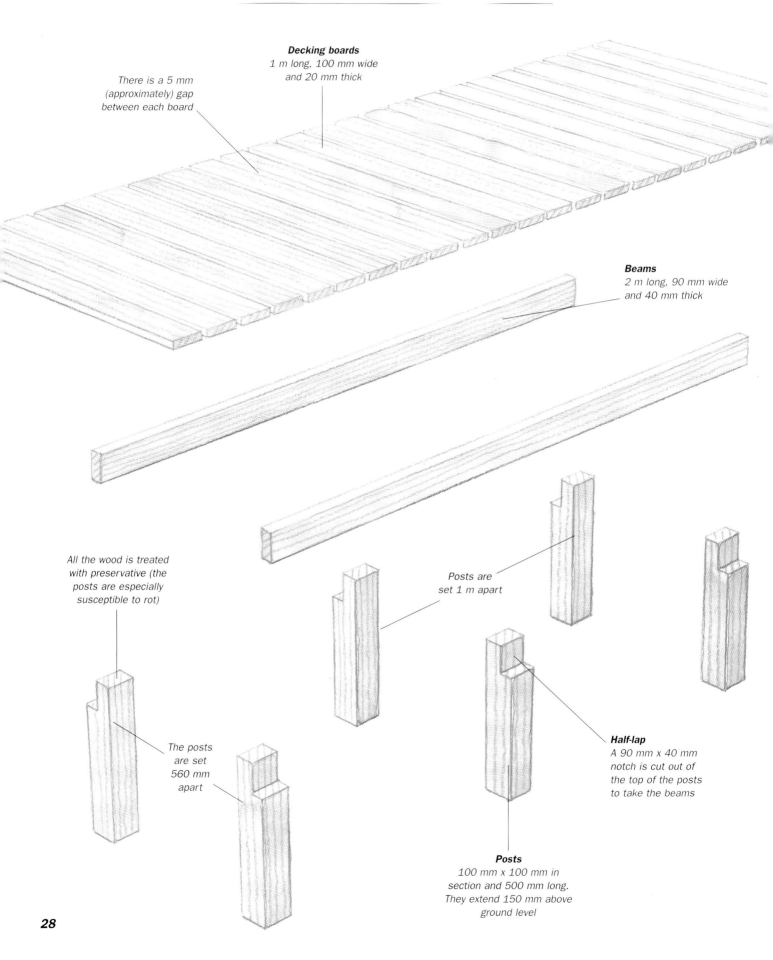

Decking boards
1 m long, 100 mm wide
and 20 mm thick

There is a 5 mm
(approximately) gap
between each board

Beams
2 m long, 90 mm wide
and 40 mm thick

All the wood is treated
with preservative (the
posts are especially
susceptible to rot)

Posts are
set 1 m apart

Half-lap
A 90 mm x 40 mm
notch is cut out of
the top of the posts
to take the beams

The posts
are set
560 mm
apart

Posts
100 mm x 100 mm in
section and 500 mm long.
They extend 150 mm above
ground level

Making the traditional boardwalk

1 Cutting the posts
Saw the 100 mm-square posts into 500 mm lengths and use the ruler and square to set out 90 mm x 40 mm half-laps. Saw across the grain to establish the length of the lap, and then use the mallet and axe to clear the waste.

2 Positioning the posts
Use the tape measure, pegs, string, spade and sledgehammer to set the posts in the ground. Place the centres of the posts 560 mm apart across the width and 1 m apart along the length of the boardwalk. They all extend 150 mm above the ground.

4 Laying the decking
Cut the 100 mm-wide decking boards into 1 m lengths and screw them in place across the beams. Centre the boards on the beams and use the 5 mm-thick offcuts to space them apart.

3 Fixing the beams
Set the beams for supporting the decking in position. Lay them on the half-laps in the posts, and fix them in place with 90 mm screws. (When fixing the beams end to end like this, make sure that they meet at the centre of the posts.)

Decking steps

All too often, steps are not built to take account of the people who use them, and are difficult to negotiate for anyone using a walking stick, a shopping trolley or a pushchair. If you want to make a grand and easy entrance, decking steps are the perfect answer – and the great advantage of this project is that they can be built over existing steps to just about any size that you wish.

★
Easy

Making time
One day
Two hours for planning and measuring, and the rest of the time for the woodwork

Considering the design

The decking steps fit over your existing steps in such a way that although they hardly change the height of the riser, they greatly increase the available standing area. You will, of course, have to modify the design to suit your particular steps, but we have made the design very flexible, so that it is easy to change.

Consider the attractions of the project. Perhaps you have an elderly relation who is unsteady on her feet and would like to be able to stand squarely on one very large step before moving to another.

Alternatively, you might simply want to give your steps a makeover to give them a more generous and inviting feel, or provide a place for pot plants by the door.

Getting started

Study the design, and then carefully measure your existing steps and see how the design needs to be tweaked to fit them. The project is for a two-step unit, but you might have to change to a one- or three-step set-up. Check whether you need to make changes to the wood sizes, or perhaps to the overall dimensions.

You will need

Tools

✔ Two portable workbenches
✔ Pencil, ruler, tape measure, marking gauge and square
✔ Crosscut saw
✔ Cordless electric drill with a cross-point screwdriver bit
✔ Drill bits to match the sizes of the screws
✔ Spirit level
✔ Electric sander

Materials

(All rough-sawn pieces of pine include excess length for wastage. All the wood is pressure-treated with preservative.)

For steps 2 m wide and 1.22 m from front to back

✔ Pine: 8 rough-sawn pieces, 2 m long, 85 mm wide and 35 mm thick (joists)
✔ Pine: 2 rough-sawn pieces, 2 m long, 75 mm square section (main vertical supports)
✔ Pine: 20 rough-sawn pieces, 2 m long, 100 mm wide and 20 mm thick (decking and riser boards)
✔ Zinc-plated, countersunk cross-headed screws: 100 x 75 mm no. 8, 200 x 50 mm no. 8

Overall dimensions and general notes

The project is a good way of improving an existing doorstep that you consider to be too narrow or unattractive. The decking steps are built over the top of the existing steps.

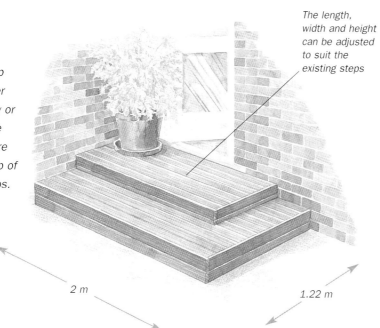

The length, width and height can be adjusted to suit the existing steps

2 m

1.22 m

Exploded view of the decking steps

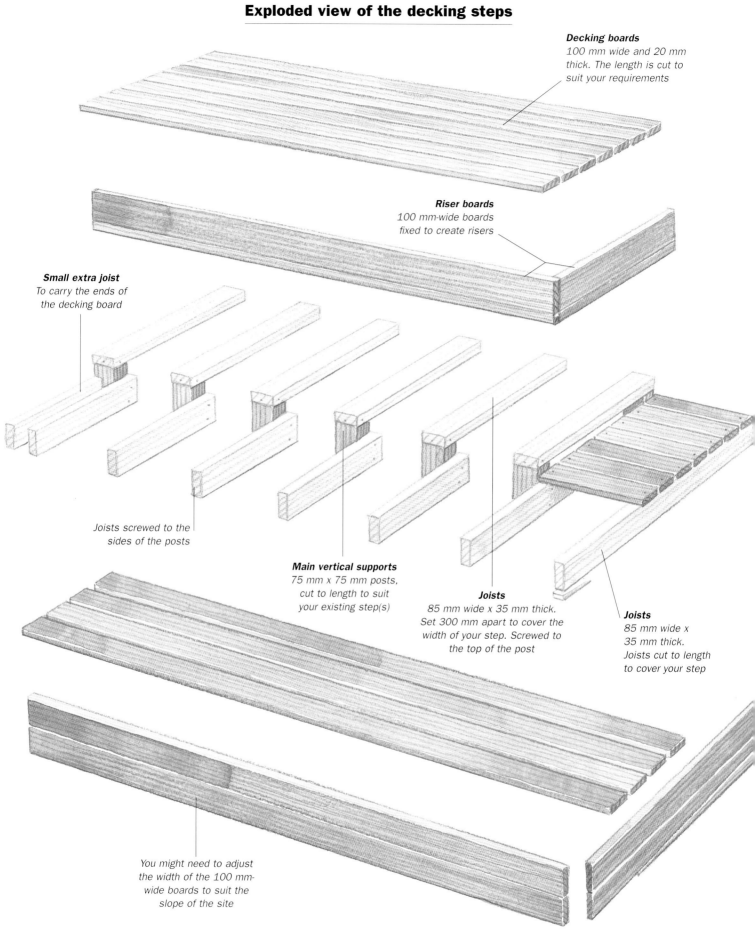

Decking boards
100 mm wide and 20 mm thick. The length is cut to suit your requirements

Riser boards
100 mm-wide boards fixed to create risers

Small extra joist
To carry the ends of the decking board

Joists screwed to the sides of the posts

Main vertical supports
75 mm x 75 mm posts, cut to length to suit your existing step(s)

Joists
85 mm wide x 35 mm thick. Set 300 mm apart to cover the width of your step. Screwed to the top of the post

Joists
85 mm wide x 35 mm thick. Joists cut to length to cover your step

You might need to adjust the width of the 100 mm-wide boards to suit the slope of the site

Making the decking steps

1 Fixing the joists
Measure your existing block of steps from front to back and cut the joists to length accordingly. Set the joists 300 mm apart (to match the full front to back measurement of your steps) and hold them in place with two lengths of decking. Use 50 mm screws.

2 Siting the frame
Place the joist frame over your steps and level it with scrap wood or whatever comes to hand. Use a spirit level to check the levels in all directions.

3 Fixing the vertical supports
Cut main vertical supports from the 75 mm square section posts. With 75 mm screws, fix them under the ends of the joists, so each joist has its own support.

4 Building the bottom step
Repeat the procedure already described to build a framework for the bottom step. Set the step at the right level and cut each main vertical support to suit the level of the ground.

5 Fitting the decking
When the two steps are in place, clad them with the decking boards, using 50 mm screws. When you come to fitting the riser boards on the bottom step, you will almost certainly have to adjust the width of the board along its length, tapering it to suit the run of the ground. Finally, sand the steps.

Japanese engawa

In a traditional Japanese garden, an *engawa* is low-level wooden decking that encircles the house, linking it to the garden and blurring the boundaries between the two. The engawa is made up of three component parts: a walkway which runs along the side of the building, a raised decking corner unit which sits at the corner of the building, and a set of steps that runs from the corner unit down to the ground.

★
Easy

Making time
One weekend
One day for making the basic framing; one day for fixing the boards and making the steps

Considering the design

By using combinations of these three basic units, you can design a scheme to suit your own requirements.

Getting started

Decide how many basic units you need. The details for the steps are in the project Garden Decking with Steps (page 58). Measure the total length of your walkway, and divide it into the 2.4 m-long modules we have given quantities for.

Overall dimensions and general notes

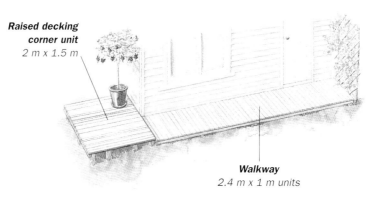

Raised decking corner unit
2 m x 1.5 m

Walkway
2.4 m x 1 m units

Using a combination of straight walkways and raised corner units, the engawa can be adapted to suit your situation.

You will need

Tools

- ✔ Pencil, ruler, tape measure and square
- ✔ Pegs and string
- ✔ Two portable workbenches
- ✔ Crosscut saw
- ✔ Cordless electric drill with a cross-point screwdriver bit
- ✔ Drill bits to match the sizes of the screws
- ✔ Craft knife
- ✔ Staple gun
- ✔ Spade and shovel
- ✔ Wheelbarrow and bucket
- ✔ Spirit level
- ✔ Electric sander
- ✔ Paintbrush

Materials

(All rough-sawn pieces of pine include excess length for wastage. All the wood is pressure-treated with preservative.)

For each 2.4 m length of walkway

- ✔ Pine: 3 rough-sawn pieces, 3 m long, 90 mm wide and 40 mm thick (joists)
- ✔ Pine: 1 rough-sawn piece, 3 m long, 75 mm square (posts)
- ✔ Pine: 8 rough-sawn pieces, 3 m long, 90 mm wide and 20 mm thick (decking boards)
- ✔ Pine: 3 rough-sawn pieces, 3 m long, 35 mm wide and 20 mm thick (decking boards)

For each 2 m x 1.5 m corner unit

- ✔ Pine: 4 rough-sawn pieces, 2 m long, 90 mm wide and 40 mm thick (joists)
- ✔ Pine: 4 rough-sawn pieces, 2 m long, 75 mm square (posts)

- ✔ Pine: 7 rough-sawn pieces, 3 m long, 90 mm wide and 20 mm thick (decking boards)
- ✔ Pine: 1 rough-sawn piece, 3 m long, 250 mm wide and 25 mm thick (decking boards)
- ✔ Pine: 3 rough-sawn pieces, 3 m long, 35 mm wide and 20 mm thick (decking boards)

General

- ✔ Zinc-plated, countersunk cross-headed screws: 200 x 75 mm no. 8, 100 x 90 mm no. 10
- ✔ Galvanized staples: 100 x 10 mm
- ✔ Concrete: 1 part (20 kg) cement, 5 parts (100 kg) ballast (for every 9 posts)
- ✔ Woven plastic weed-stop sheeting (large enough for the total decking area of the ground-level walkways)
- ✔ Exterior-grade matt white paint

Exploded view of the Japanese engawa

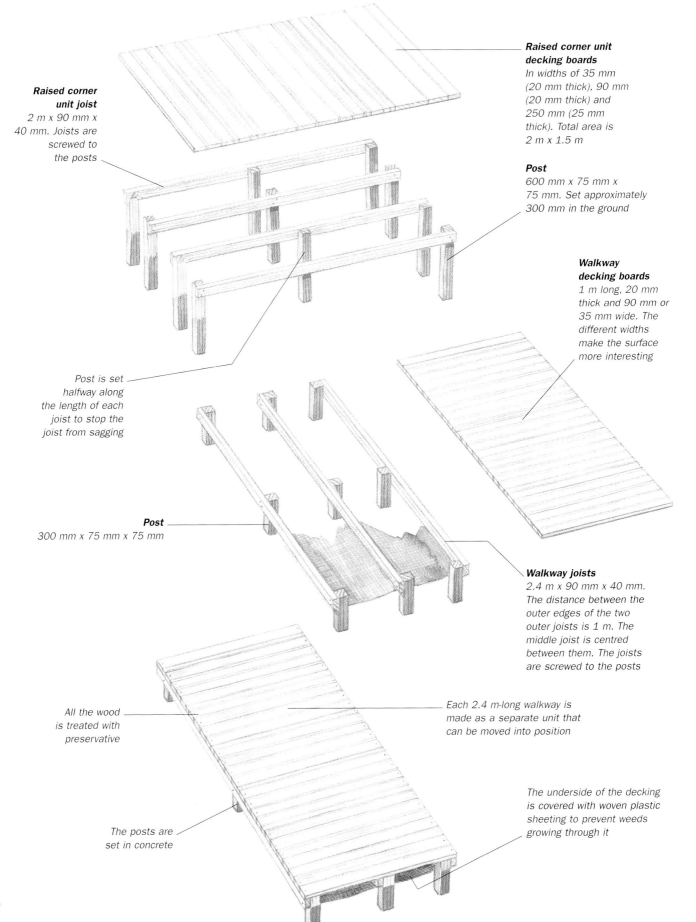

Raised corner unit joist
2 m x 90 mm x 40 mm. Joists are screwed to the posts

Raised corner unit decking boards
In widths of 35 mm (20 mm thick), 90 mm (20 mm thick) and 250 mm (25 mm thick). Total area is 2 m x 1.5 m

Post
600 mm x 75 mm x 75 mm. Set approximately 300 mm in the ground

Walkway decking boards
1 m long, 20 mm thick and 90 mm or 35 mm wide. The different widths make the surface more interesting

Post is set halfway along the length of each joist to stop the joist from sagging

Post
300 mm x 75 mm x 75 mm

Walkway joists
2.4 m x 90 mm x 40 mm. The distance between the outer edges of the two outer joists is 1 m. The middle joist is centred between them. The joists are screwed to the posts

Each 2.4 m-long walkway is made as a separate unit that can be moved into position

All the wood is treated with preservative

The underside of the decking is covered with woven plastic sheeting to prevent weeds growing through it

The posts are set in concrete

Making the Japanese engawa

1 Building the walkway frame
Take three 2.4 m lengths of wood for the joists, and position them as shown on the drawing to make the basic three-joist frame. Screw a 1 m-long piece of 20 mm-thick decking board at each end to hold the frame square, using 75 mm screws.

2 Fixing the plastic
Turn the frame upside-down, and cut a piece of the woven plastic sheet to fit. Staple it to what will be the underside of the joists.

3 Screwing on the posts
Cut nine 300 mm lengths of 75 mm square-section wood and screw them to the joists with 90 mm screws to make the posts (cut the plastic to fit around each post). Put one at each end of the joists, and one halfway along their length to provide a central support.

4 Concreting the posts
Set the frame on the ground and establish the position of the posts. Dig holes 210 mm deep. (The walkway sits at ground level.) Make a dryish mix of concrete, put it in the holes and lower the frame into place. Tamp the concrete around the posts with a piece of wood.

5 Building other frames
Follow the same procedures for all the walkway frames, all the while using the spirit level to ensure that the frames are level with each other. Build the raised decking corner units in the same way, concreting the 600 mm-long posts into holes 300 mm deep.

6 Fixing the decking on all frames
Screw the decking boards across the joists with 75 mm screws. To complete the engawa, sand down the whole structure. Mix the white paint with a good quantity of water to make a thin wash, and give the engawa two coats. See page 58 for how to build the steps.

Circular patio

The circular patio is intriguing to look at – reminiscent of a waterwheel, or maybe part of a windmill. Its arresting appearance makes the perfect setting for a water feature or a flower display, and the rugged decking provides a good, level surface for all manner of other garden activities. You can easily save on material costs by using salvaged wood, such as old floorboards, if necessary.

★
Easy

**Making time
One weekend**
One day for building the hexagonal frames; one day for putting it together and finishing

Considering the design

The patio is constructed from wedge-shaped segments cut from eighteen pine planks, measuring 1.05 m long, 250 mm wide and 25 mm thick. This provides 35 wedges and allows a spare one left over for good measure. The diameter of the patio is about 2.5 m.

We set the patio in an existing circle of pea gravel. If you want to create a similar gravel area specifically for your patio, you will need about eight wheelbarrow loads of fine pea gravel. The wedge-shaped decking boards are screwed to three hexagonal under-frames. When the whole patio construction is in place, the frames are held secure by the gravel, and the boards are supported and displayed to their best advantage.

Getting started

Have a look at your site, and decide whereabouts you want the patio to be placed. Use pegs and string to set out a circular area something over 2.5 m in diameter, and cover it with gravel. Edge the circle with a material of your choice. We have used log roll edging, and arranged a few cobbles in the space between the patio and the edging.

You will need

Tools

- Pencil, ruler, tape measure and square
- Pegs and string
- Two portable workbenches
- Electric mitre saw
- Rip saw
- Cordless electric drill with a cross-point screwdriver bit
- Drill bits to match the sizes of the screws
- Rake

Materials

(All rough-sawn pieces of pine include excess length for wastage. All the wood is pressure-treated with preservative.)

For a patio 2.5 m in diameter

- Pine: 9 rough-sawn pieces, 2.1 m long, 250 mm wide and 25 mm thick (wedge boards)
- Pine: 8 rough-sawn pieces, 2 m long, 75 mm wide and 30 mm thick (hexagonal frames)
- Zinc-plated, countersunk cross-headed screws: 50 x 75 mm no. 10, 200 x 50 mm no. 8

Overall dimensions and general notes

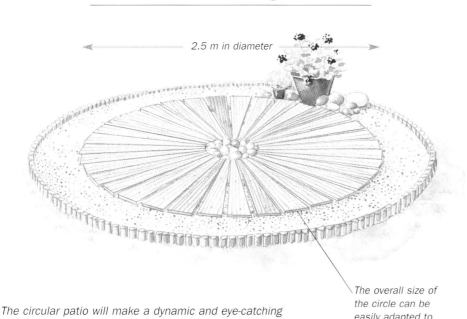

2.5 m in diameter

The overall size of the circle can be easily adapted to suit any garden

The circular patio will make a dynamic and eye-catching feature, whether in a small town plot or a larger garden.

Exploded view of the circular patio

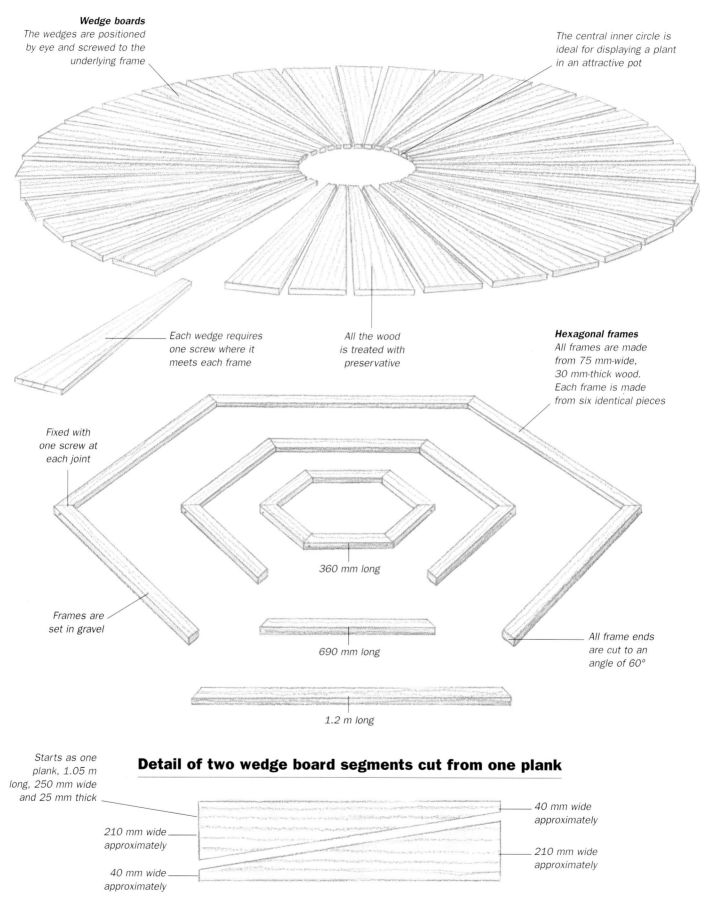

Wedge boards
The wedges are positioned by eye and screwed to the underlying frame

The central inner circle is ideal for displaying a plant in an attractive pot

Each wedge requires one screw where it meets each frame

All the wood is treated with preservative

Hexagonal frames
All frames are made from 75 mm-wide, 30 mm-thick wood. Each frame is made from six identical pieces

Fixed with one screw at each joint

Frames are set in gravel

360 mm long

690 mm long

All frame ends are cut to an angle of 60°

1.2 m long

Detail of two wedge board segments cut from one plank

Starts as one plank, 1.05 m long, 250 mm wide and 25 mm thick

40 mm wide approximately

210 mm wide approximately

210 mm wide approximately

40 mm wide approximately

Making the circular patio

1 Cutting the wedges
Cut the wedge boards into 1.05 m lengths, and mark them off into two parts, as shown on page 40. Use the rip saw to cut them diagonally along their length, so that you have two wedges.

2 Cutting the frames
Mark out the pieces that make the three hexagonal frames. Set the mitre saw to make a 60°/30° cut and saw the wood to length. You need six identical lengths for each hexagon.

3 Screwing the frames
Lay out the pieces for each frame and fix them together with 75 mm screws. Drill pilot holes before screwing so that you do not split the wood.

4 Positioning the frames
Position the three frames, one within another, on the gravel circle. Stand back and look at them from several angles to ensure that they are centred and correctly aligned, and then rake the gravel level with the top of the frames.

5 Fixing the wedges
Set all the wedge-shaped boards in place. Check by eye and make adjustments until you are happy with the arrangement, then fix them with 50 mm screws, using one screw for each board–frame intersection.

Country walk path

This sweeping path looks good in both country and urban settings, and will remain dry, firm and level despite assault by the weather and wear and tear by humans. It is simplicity itself – there is no need to mix concrete for securing posts or to lay plastic sheet to stop the growth of weeds. If you like the notion of a low-key path, and you want to build it quickly and easily, this is a good project to try.

★
Easy

Making time
One weekend for a
6 m path
One day for trenches and cutting wood; one day for construction

Considering the design

The path measures approximately 1 m wide. It is made from two types of post – 500 mm lengths of turned, round-section wood (150 mm in diameter) for the edging, and 500 mm lengths of 100 mm square-section wood for the walkway blocks. Once the edging is in place, the walkway blocks are carefully positioned about 50 mm apart on a base of large-size gravel or shingle, and then the spaces in and around the blocks are topped up with fine pea gravel. The blocks are firm and level, making a good, safe path, which is perfect for all users of the garden and their activities, whether it is strolling, pushing a wheelbarrow, or playing.

Getting started

Use the tape measure, pegs and string to set out the route of the path. Note that you need six round-section posts (1 m long), and three square-section posts (1 m long) for each metre length of path (all posts will be cut in half). Clear the route of plants, and dig out the area to a depth of 200 mm. Establish the position of the two trenches.

You will need

Tools

- ✓ Pencil, ruler, tape measure and square
- ✓ Spade and shovel
- ✓ Two portable workbenches
- ✓ Crosscut saw
- ✓ Sledgehammer
- ✓ Rake
- ✓ Wheelbarrow

Materials

(All rough-sawn pieces of pine include excess length for wastage. All the wood is pressure-treated with preservative.)

For 1 m of path, 1 m wide

- ✓ Pine: 6 round-section turned posts, 1 m long, 150 mm in diameter (posts)
- ✓ Pine: 3 rough-sawn pieces, 1 m long, 100 mm square section (walkway blocks)
- ✓ Shingle: 1 wheelbarrow load of large-size shingle
- ✓ Pea gravel: 1 wheelbarrow load

Overall dimensions and general notes

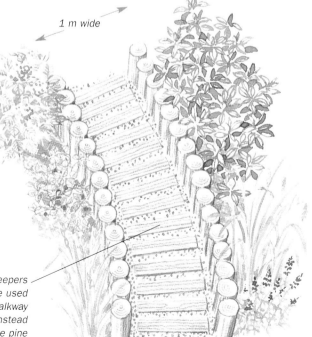

1 m wide

This is a good project for anywhere in a town or country garden, but it will look at its best winding through a lush, forest-like area.

Railway sleepers could be used for the walkway blocks instead of the pine

Exploded view of the country walk path

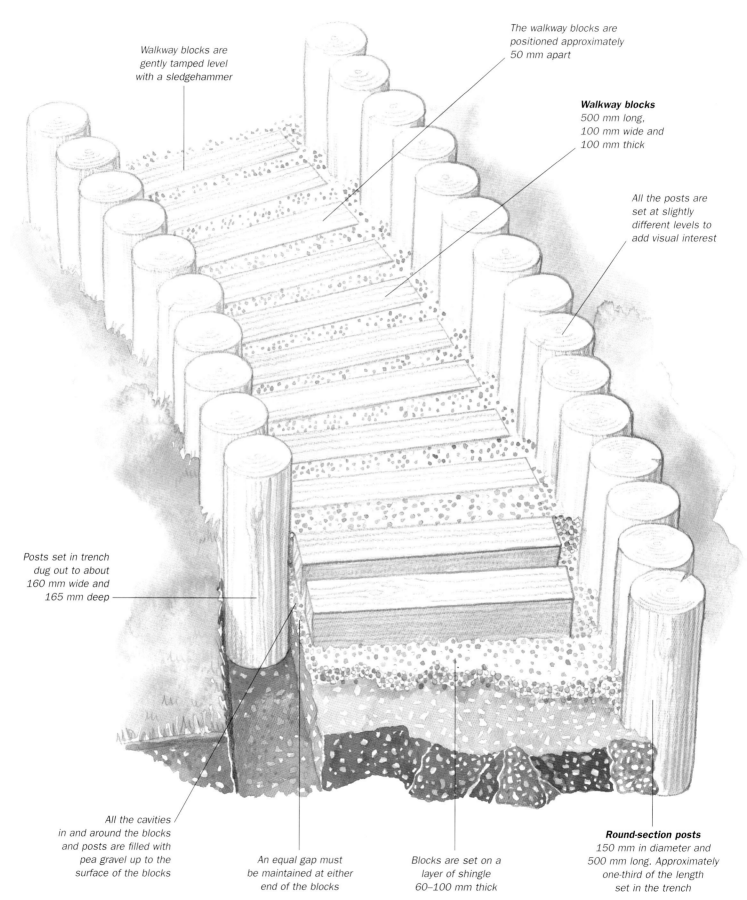

Walkway blocks are gently tamped level with a sledgehammer

The walkway blocks are positioned approximately 50 mm apart

Walkway blocks
500 mm long, 100 mm wide and 100 mm thick

All the posts are set at slightly different levels to add visual interest

Posts set in trench dug out to about 160 mm wide and 165 mm deep

All the cavities in and around the blocks and posts are filled with pea gravel up to the surface of the blocks

An equal gap must be maintained at either end of the blocks

Blocks are set on a layer of shingle 60–100 mm thick

Round-section posts
150 mm in diameter and 500 mm long. Approximately one-third of the length set in the trench

Making the country walk path

1 Setting out the path

Use the tape measure, pegs and string to set out the route of the path. Dig out the area to a depth of 200 mm and a total width of 1 m. Dig a trench along one side of the path about 160 mm wide and 165 mm deep and set in a row of 500 mm-long round-section posts.

2 Completing the posts

Repeat the procedure for the other side of the path. Use the excavated earth to fill around the posts and to generally level the area. Tamp with the sledgehammer.

3 Spreading shingle

Shovel a layer of shingle over the ground between the posts, and then spread and level it with the rake, making it 60–100 mm thick. Tamp the shingle into the earth until it is firm underfoot.

4 Laying the walkway blocks

Take the 500 mm-long walkway blocks of 100 mm square-section wood and place them on the gravel, about 50 mm apart and centred within the width of the path. Adjust them so that they radiate around the curves. Lay the pea gravel.

Japanese bridge

The Japanese bridge allows you to cross over a narrow expanse of water. It is made by spanning the water with two beams 100 mm in diameter, which are covered with 85 mm-wide, 40 mm-thick decking. There is a handrail to one side of the bridge made from bamboo. The handrail posts are bolted directly to the side of one beam, and braced and triangulated to the underside of the other.

★ ★
Intermediate

Making time
One weekend
One day for the main beams and decking, and one day for the bamboo handrail

Considering the design

The bridge is 3.6 m long – if you wish, you can make it shorter, but for reasons of safety it cannot be made any longer. The handrail is fixed to the posts with mortise and tenon joints, pegs are driven into the sides of the posts, and then the joints are lashed together with cord.

Getting started

Clear the foliage from the bank sides and check that the ground is firm. Inspect the main beams to make sure that they are free from splits and deep knots.

Overall dimensions and general notes

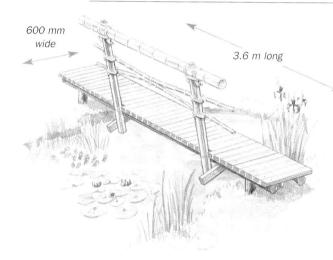

600 mm wide

3.6 m long

We have chosen to build this bridge over a pond, but it would also look good built over a dry "river" of gravel in the Japanese tradition.

You will need

Tools

- Pencil, ruler, tape measure and square
- Pegs and string
- Two portable workbenches
- Crosscut saw
- Spade and sledgehammer
- Claw hammer
- Axe
- Wrench to fit the bolts
- Cordless electric drill with a cross-point screwdriver bit, 25 mm flat bit
- Drill bits to match the sizes of the screws, nails and bolts
- Electric jigsaw
- Electric sander

Materials

(All rough-sawn pieces of pine include excess length for wastage. All the wood is pressure-treated with preservative. Nails are purchased to the nearest kg measure.)

For a bridge 3.6 m long and 600 mm wide

- Pine: 2 round-section pieces, 4 m long, 100 mm in diameter (main beams)
- Pine: 2 round-section pieces, 3 m long, 100 mm in diameter (support piles, handrail posts and rail pegs)
- Pine: 15 rough-sawn pieces, 2 m long, 85 mm wide and 40 mm thick (decking and bracing)
- Pine: 1 rough-sawn piece, 4 m long, 30 mm wide and 20 mm thick (temporary batten)

- Bamboo: 1 piece, 3 m long, 100 mm in diameter (handrail)
- Bamboo: 2 pieces, 3 m long (secondary rails)
- Cord: 20 m of heavy-duty natural fibre cord (for binding the joints)
- Nails: 1 kg of 150 mm x 6 mm (for fixing the main beams to the piles)
- Nails: 2 kg of 125 mm x 5.6 mm (for fixing the decking to the beams)
- Zinc-plated, countersunk cross-headed screws: 50 x 90 mm no. 10
- Coach bolts: 2 x 250 mm long, with nuts and washers to fit

Exploded view of the Japanese bridge

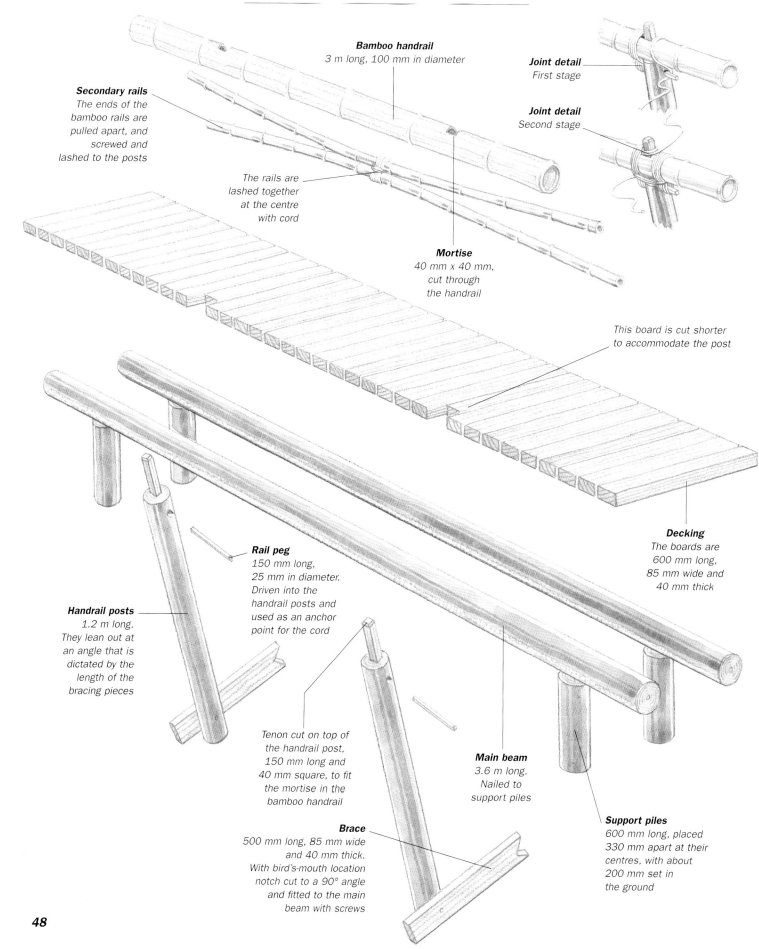

Bamboo handrail
3 m long, 100 mm in diameter

Joint detail
First stage

Joint detail
Second stage

Secondary rails
The ends of the bamboo rails are pulled apart, and screwed and lashed to the posts

The rails are lashed together at the centre with cord

Mortise
40 mm x 40 mm, cut through the handrail

This board is cut shorter to accommodate the post

Decking
The boards are 600 mm long, 85 mm wide and 40 mm thick

Rail peg
150 mm long, 25 mm in diameter. Driven into the handrail posts and used as an anchor point for the cord

Handrail posts
1.2 m long. They lean out at an angle that is dictated by the length of the bracing pieces

Tenon cut on top of the handrail post, 150 mm long and 40 mm square, to fit the mortise in the bamboo handrail

Main beam
3.6 m long. Nailed to support piles

Support piles
600 mm long, placed 330 mm apart at their centres, with about 200 mm set in the ground

Brace
500 mm long, 85 mm wide and 40 mm thick. With bird's-mouth location notch cut to a 90° angle and fitted to the main beam with screws

Making the Japanese bridge

1 Fixing the main beams

Cut four 600 mm-long support piles and dig them in at either side of the water, so that they are level and 330 mm apart at their centres, and 400 mm above ground level. Nail the main beams directly to the top of the posts with 150 mm nails.

2 Fixing the decking

Centre and nail one 600 mm-long decking board at either end of the main beams. Nail the temporary batten to the ends of the boards to act as a guide, and then nail all the decking boards in place. Leave two gaps for the handrail posts. Use 125 mm nails throughout.

3 Making the handrail

Cut the handrail posts to length. Use the saw and axe to cut tenons 150 mm long and 40 mm square on what will be the top end of each post. Use coach bolts to bolt the handrail posts securely to the main beams (see illustration, step 4).

4 Bracing

Cut the two braces to length. Cut a right-angled bird's-mouth location notch on one end of each brace. Screw the braces between the end of the posts and the underside of the beams.

5 Fixing the handrail

Mark in the position of the mortise holes on the bamboo handrail, and cut them out with the drill and jigsaw. Sit the handrail on the tenons. Drill holes and bang in the rail pegs, and lash the joints with the cord.

6 Adding secondary rails

Lash the two bamboo secondary rails together at the centre, and drill and screw them to the posts. Finally, bind over the screws with the cord. Sand everything to a good finish.

Planter tubs

Planter tubs make a great addition to any outdoor space. They can be filled with an ever-changing display to inject colour into the garden throughout the year. Wood has an instant appeal when combined with plants – as a natural material, it instantly harmonizes. These planters are built with variously cut and curved pickets, in folksy style, or with square pickets topped with a mitred frame, for a clean, modern look.

Making time
One weekend
One day for building the frames and cutting the pickets, and one day for putting together

Considering the design

Each of the three planters is built from two horizontal frames, with pickets fixed vertically to the outside so that the frames are hidden from view.

We have made a large planter with square pickets, trimmed on top with a decorative mitred frame, a medium planter with rounded pickets, and a small planter with pointed pickets. If you follow our suggestions exactly, this assortment of styles will provide an eclectic look for your patio. Alternatively, you can opt for a more traditional look and make a set of three planters to the same design.

The frames are built from battens, 35 mm wide and 20 mm thick, the pickets are cut from boards, 70 mm wide and 16 mm thick, and the right-angled corner fillet pieces are cut from wood 60 mm wide and 30 mm thick.

Getting started

If you want to vary the design, shape, size and quantity of the planters, sit down with a pencil and paper and work out the materials, and then order the wood accordingly. You have to decide on the design of the top, the total height, and the length and width of the sides.

You will need

Tools

- ✔ Pencil, ruler, compass, tape measure, bevel gauge and square
- ✔ Two portable workbenches
- ✔ Crosscut saw
- ✔ Cordless electric drill with a cross-point screwdriver bit
- ✔ Drill bits to match the sizes of the screws
- ✔ Claw hammer
- ✔ Electric jigsaw and electric sander

Materials

(All rough-sawn pieces of pine include excess length for wastage. All the wood is pressure-treated with preservative. Make sure this is of a type that is not harmful to plants.)

For a large, medium and small planter tub

- ✔ Pine: 5 rough-sawn pieces, 3 m long, 35 mm wide and 20 mm thick (frames)
- ✔ Pine: 1 rough-sawn piece, 2 m long, 60 mm wide and 30 mm thick (corner fillets)
- ✔ Pine: 15 rough-sawn pieces, 3 m long, 70 mm wide and 16 mm thick (pickets, decorative mitred frame, floorboards)
- ✔ Zinc-plated, countersunk cross-headed screws: 200 x 30 mm no. 8, 200 x 50 mm no. 8
- ✔ Galvanized nails: 2 kg of 40 mm-long nails

Overall dimensions and general notes

Medium planter
510 mm square and 540 mm high

Large planter
910 mm x 585 mm x 350 mm high

Small planter
510 mm square and 410 mm high

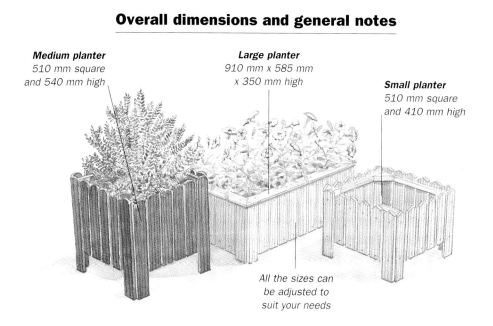

All the sizes can be adjusted to suit your needs

Planter tubs can brighten up an area of decking, a patio, or a balcony garden. They can be filled directly with earth; alternatively, plants in pots can be arranged in them.

Exploded view of the large planter tub

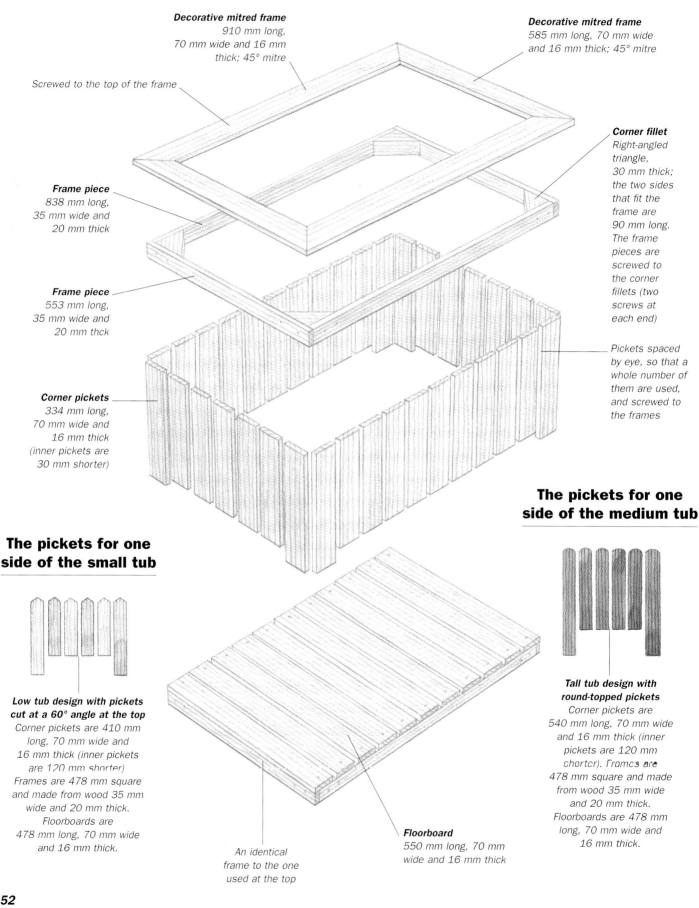

Decorative mitred frame
*910 mm long,
70 mm wide and 16 mm
thick; 45° mitre*

Screwed to the top of the frame

Decorative mitred frame
*585 mm long, 70 mm wide
and 16 mm thick; 45° mitre*

Corner fillet
*Right-angled
triangle,
30 mm thick;
the two sides
that fit the
frame are
90 mm long.
The frame
pieces are
screwed to
the corner
fillets (two
screws at
each end)*

Frame piece
*838 mm long,
35 mm wide and
20 mm thick*

Frame piece
*553 mm long,
35 mm wide and
20 mm thck*

Corner pickets
*334 mm long,
70 mm wide and
16 mm thick
(inner pickets are
30 mm shorter)*

*Pickets spaced
by eye, so that a
whole number of
them are used,
and screwed to
the frames*

The pickets for one side of the small tub

**Low tub design with pickets
cut at a 60° angle at the top**
*Corner pickets are 410 mm
long, 70 mm wide and
16 mm thick (inner pickets
are 120 mm shorter)
Frames are 478 mm square
and made from wood 35 mm
wide and 20 mm thick.
Floorboards are
478 mm long, 70 mm wide
and 16 mm thick.*

The pickets for one side of the medium tub

**Tall tub design with
round-topped pickets**
*Corner pickets are
540 mm long, 70 mm wide
and 16 mm thick (inner
pickets are 120 mm
shorter). Frames are
478 mm square and made
from wood 35 mm wide
and 20 mm thick.
Floorboards are 478 mm
long, 70 mm wide and
16 mm thick.*

*An identical
frame to the one
used at the top*

Floorboard
*550 mm long, 70 mm
wide and 16 mm thick*

Making the planter tubs

1 Constructing the frames
Cut the component parts for the frames, and the corner fillets, to length. Set the parts together, drill pilot holes and fix them with 50 mm screws. Make two frames for each tub.

2 Fixing the corner pickets
Cut the corner pickets to length and screw them to the corners of the top frame with 30 mm screws. Note how the extended length of the corner pickets creates the leg feature.

3 Making the floor
Cut the floorboards to length and nail them to the bottom frame. Drill pilot holes for the nails, to avoid splitting the wood. Space the floorboards by eye so that you use a complete number to cover the frame.

4 Putting together
Screw the bottom frame to the corner pickets. Check that the structure is square and screw all the inner pickets in place on both frames. Use 30 mm screws throughout. Space the pickets by eye so that you use a complete number to cover each side of the planter.

5 Decorative frame for large tub
The large planter has a decorative mitred frame on the top. Cut pieces of wood to fit both the length and width of the tub. Mitre the corners with the jigsaw and screw the resultant frame to the top of the tub with 30 mm screws, to cover the tops of the pickets.

6 Shaped pickets
If you are going to fit shaped pickets (curved for the medium planter and pointed for the small planter), draw curves or mark centre points on the pickets with the compass. Use the jigsaw to fret out the profile. Finally, sand all the planters to a good finish.

Chequerboard decking patio

★ ★
Intermediate

The good thing about the chequerboard patio is its flexibility. The design allows it to be square, rectilinear, castellated, or just about any shape that inspires you, as long as the sum total shape can be made up from a square grid. The chequerboard grid construction also permits you to miss out selected squares in order to plant flowers, or site a bench seat, sandpit, water feature, tree or area of soft grass.

Making time
One weekend
One day for building the gridded frame, and the rest of the time for fitting the decking

Considering the design

The frame is set face down on a bed of gravel. It is made up of eight joists spaced 365 mm apart in one direction, topped by a second layer set at right angles in the other direction. The resulting grid is secured and held square by screwing 300 mm-long filler pieces to the bottom layer. Finally, the decking boards are simply screwed to the gridded frame.

The techniques are straightforward – there are no difficult-to-use tools involved or complex jointing to do – but this very simplicity calls for extra care and effort at the designing and planning stage in order to get good results.

Getting started

Look at your site and decide whether you want the patio to follow the dimensions of the project (2.62 m square). Use a tape measure, pegs and string to mark it out. Transfer the shape to gridded paper, so that the joists are 365 mm apart at their centres. Work out how much wood is needed if dimensions have altered.

You will need

Tools

✔ Pencil, ruler, tape measure, square, bevel gauge, gridded paper

✔ Pegs and string

✔ Spade and wheelbarrow

✔ Cordless electric drill with a cross-point screwdriver bit

✔ Drill bits to match the sizes of the screws

✔ Crosscut saw

✔ Two portable workbenches

✔ Electric sander

✔ Paintbrush

Materials

(All rough-sawn pieces of pine include excess length for wastage. All the wood is pressure-treated with preservative.)

For a patio 2.62 m square

✔ Pine: 24 rough-sawn pieces, 3 m long, 65 mm wide and 30 mm thick (frame and filler pieces)

✔ Pine: 33 rough-sawn pieces, 3 m long, 75 mm wide and 16 mm thick (decking boards)

✔ Zinc-plated, countersunk cross-headed screws: 100 x 55 mm no. 8, 200 x 35 mm no. 8

✔ Woven plastic sheeting: 3 m x 3 m

✔ Gravel: 10 wheelbarrow loads

✔ Exterior-grade decking paint

Overall dimensions and general notes

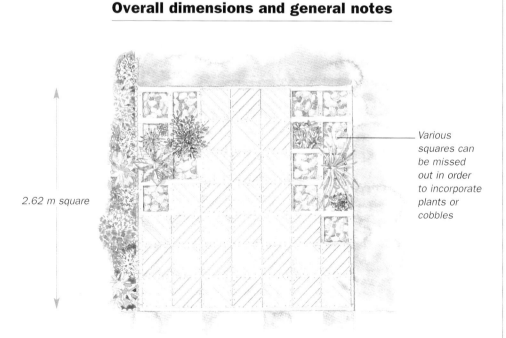

2.62 m square

Various squares can be missed out in order to incorporate plants or cobbles

This is an excellent project when space is limited. The patio can also be used to reduce the monotony of a large area of lawn. It could even be painted in bold colours.

Exploded view of the chequerboard decking patio

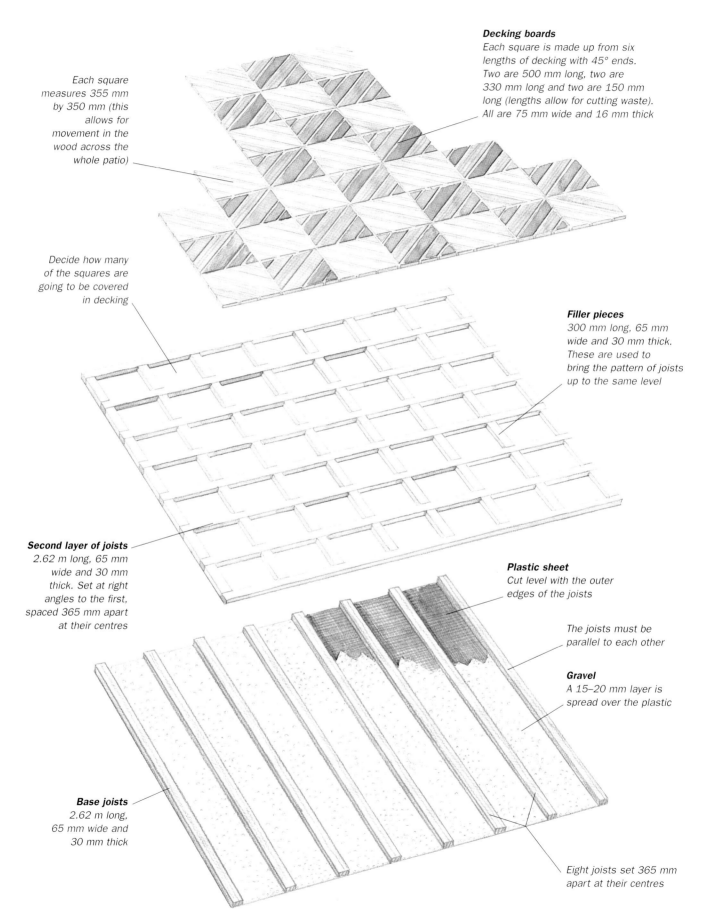

Decking boards
Each square is made up from six lengths of decking with 45° ends. Two are 500 mm long, two are 330 mm long and two are 150 mm long (lengths allow for cutting waste). All are 75 mm wide and 16 mm thick

Each square measures 355 mm by 350 mm (this allows for movement in the wood across the whole patio)

Decide how many of the squares are going to be covered in decking

Filler pieces
300 mm long, 65 mm wide and 30 mm thick. These are used to bring the pattern of joists up to the same level

Second layer of joists
2.62 m long, 65 mm wide and 30 mm thick. Set at right angles to the first, spaced 365 mm apart at their centres

Plastic sheet
Cut level with the outer edges of the joists

The joists must be parallel to each other

Gravel
A 15–20 mm layer is spread over the plastic

Base joists
2.62 m long, 65 mm wide and 30 mm thick

Eight joists set 365 mm apart at their centres

Making the chequerboard decking patio

1 Placing the base joists
Spread the plastic sheeting over the site and cover it with a 15–20 mm layer of washed gravel. Take eight joists and position them side by side, so that they are parallel to each other and set 365 mm apart at the centres.

2 Placing the second layer
Take eight more joists and position them on top of the base joists in the manner just described, so that they are side by side in a grid pattern and set 365 mm apart at the centres. Run 55 mm screws down through the intersections to fix the layers together.

3 Adding filler pieces
Cut 300 mm lengths of the 65 mm x 30 mm wood to make filler pieces for the grid. Place these over the visible parts of the first layer of joists to bring them up to the level of the second layer. Screw the filler pieces in place with 55 mm screws.

4 Cutting the decking
Look at the gridded frame, decide on the edge profile and where you want the planting holes to occur, and calculate how many squares you need to cover with decking. Cut and mitre six lengths of decking board (see page 56 for measurements) for each square.

5 Fitting the decking
Set the decking boards on the frame in the pattern and configuration that you have planned, and fix them in place with 35 mm screws. Sand the structure. Finally, thin the paint with water to create a colourwash, and brush on.

Garden decking with steps

★ ★
Intermediate

Decking is great for a sloping site. You don't have the task of moving vast quantities of earth to create a level area, because you simply float the decking over the problem by adjusting the length of the legs to accommodate the slope of the ground. Once the decking is in place, you will suddenly be able to see the garden in a whole new light – the experience is rather like sitting on a flying carpet.

Making time
Two weekends
One day for casting the foot pads, two days for building the decking, one day for finishing

Considering the design

This large, square platform has a post at each corner, and a small flight of steps centred on one side. The platform frame is bolted directly to the legs, which are socketed into concrete pads.

Getting started

Measure out the site, clear the ground and establish where the concrete pads will go. Decide where you want the steps to be fixed. Arrange the wood in ordered stacks, and recruit friends for future help at the levelling stage, when you will have to bolt the frame to the legs.

Overall dimensions and general notes

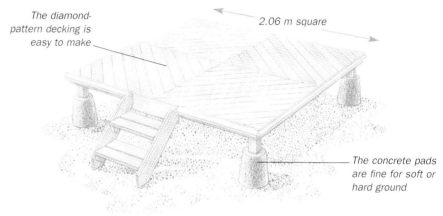

The diamond-pattern decking is easy to make

2.06 m square

The concrete pads are fine for soft or hard ground

This decking is suitable for a level or sloping site (the lengths of the posts are varied accordingly) and is ideal for sunbathing or as the site for a table and a couple of chairs.

You will need

Tools

- ✔ Pencil, ruler, tape measure, marking gauge and square
- ✔ Two portable workbenches
- ✔ Crosscut saw, spade, shovel
- ✔ Wheelbarrow, bucket, spirit level
- ✔ Cordless electric drill with a cross-point screwdriver bit
- ✔ Drill bits to match the sizes of the nails, screws and bolts
- ✔ Claw hammer, ratchet spanner
- ✔ Electric sander

Materials

(All pieces of rough-sawn wood include excess length for wastage. All the wood is pressure-treated with preservative.)

For decking 2.06 m square and about 500 mm high

- ✔ Pine: 1 rough-sawn piece, 2 m long, 75 mm square section (leg posts, support blocks and moulding blocks)
- ✔ Pine: 10 rough-sawn pieces, 2 m long, 70 mm wide and 40 mm thick (framework and joists)
- ✔ Pine: 25 pieces of planed, grooved decking boards, 2 m long, 95 mm wide and 25 mm thick (floor)
- ✔ Pine: 4 pieces of rough-sawn, pitch-top fence capping, 2 m long, 65 mm wide and 30 mm thick (frame trim)

- ✔ Pine: 1 rough-sawn piece, 3 m long, 150 mm wide, 20 mm thick (stringers)
- ✔ Pine: grooved decking, 3 m long, 120 mm wide, 35 mm thick (treads)
- ✔ Pine: 1 rough-sawn piece, 1 m long, 65 mm wide, 30 mm thick (brackets)
- ✔ Zinc-plated coach bolts with washers and nuts to fit: 8 x 150 mm
- ✔ Zinc-plated, countersunk cross-headed screws: 300 x 100 mm no. 8, 300 x 75 mm no. 10, 50 x 50 mm no. 8
- ✔ Steel nails: 1 kg, 125 mm x 5.6 mm
- ✔ Concrete: 1 part (25 kg) cement, 2 parts (50 kg) sharp sand, 3 parts (75 kg) aggregate
- ✔ Six plastic flowerpots: about 250 mm high, 235 mm wide at the rim, and 175 mm wide at the base
- ✔ Sticky tape

Exploded view of the garden decking with steps

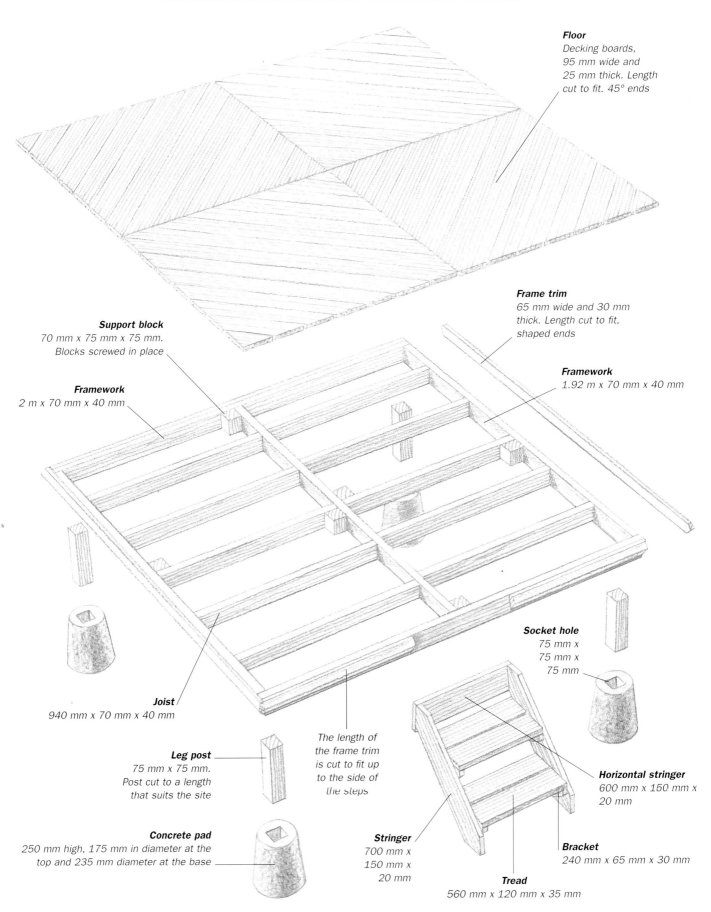

Floor
Decking boards, 95 mm wide and 25 mm thick. Length cut to fit. 45° ends

Frame trim
65 mm wide and 30 mm thick. Length cut to fit, shaped ends

Support block
70 mm x 75 mm x 75 mm. Blocks screwed in place

Framework
2 m x 70 mm x 40 mm

Framework
1.92 m x 70 mm x 40 mm

Socket hole
75 mm x 75 mm x 75 mm

Joist
940 mm x 70 mm x 40 mm

The length of the frame trim is cut to fit up to the side of the steps

Leg post
75 mm x 75 mm. Post cut to a length that suits the site

Horizontal stringer
600 mm x 150 mm x 20 mm

Concrete pad
250 mm high, 175 mm in diameter at the top and 235 mm diameter at the base

Stringer
700 mm x 150 mm x 20 mm

Bracket
240 mm x 65 mm x 30 mm

Tread
560 mm x 120 mm x 35 mm

Making the garden decking with steps

1 Making the concrete pads
Cut six 75 mm-long moulding blocks from the 75 mm-square wood and set one in the bottom of each plastic flowerpot. Cover the hole at the bottom with sticky tape and fill the pots with concrete. (Two extra pots have been allowed in case of mistakes.)

2 Making the framework
Cut the wood for the framework (see page 60). Build a frame 2 m square, with a central joist crossing between opposite sides. Screw on 75 mm-square support blocks (see diagram) to strengthen the primary T-junction joints. Use 100 mm screws throughout.

3 Fixing the secondary joists
Set the secondary joists in place in each quarter of the frame – so that they are a tight wedge fit – and spike them in place with nails. Ease the concrete foot pads out of the flowerpots and remove the wood to reveal the sockets.

4 Setting the frame on its legs
With friends to help, cut one post for each leg, and push them into the sockets in the concrete pads. Bolt the legs inside the corners of the frame, and check that the frame is level. Saw the top of the leg posts level with the top edge of the frame.

5 Making the steps
Construct the steps from the treads, stringers and brackets, and fix to the frame, using 75 mm screws. Cut the frame trim to fit, shaping the ends to create neat corners to cover the sawn ends of the decking. Screw it in place on the frame with 50 mm screws.

6 Making the floor
Cut the decking boards for the floor to size and screw them to the top surface of the joists with 75 mm screws. Finally, use the sander to rub all the sawn ends to a slightly rounded, splinter-free finish.

Bench seat and safety rail

If you fancy having a bench seat to put on an area of decking, try this project. Because it is potentially dangerous if a bench is placed near the edge of the decking, we have designed a rail to act as a safety barrier. The rail and baluster design can easily be modified to match the style of existing decking. If you wish, the bench can be bolted to both the decking and the rail to make an extra-strong structure.

★ ★
Intermediate

Making time
Two weekends
Two days for the bench seat and two days for the rail

Considering the design

Both items have been designed so that they can be made from off-the-shelf sections. In many of our projects, function follows form, meaning that the way the design looks in the garden is as least as important as the way the project functions, so that it doesn't matter too much if you make changes to the design.

However in this instance, function is all-important, and both the bench and rail must be safe before any other considerations. (This is especially true for rails. They must be just the right height, and fitted so that they can stand a fair amount of wear and tear.) So you must think very carefully before you make any major structural changes to the designs.

Finally, we used exterior-grade paint to add an attractive finish to the design.

Getting started

Look at your decking and consider the best site for the bench and rail. The weight of the bench must be equally distributed over the joists of the decking, and the rail must be bolted to one or more of the primary joists. We have fixed rails to two sides of a relatively low decking patio, but if you have an area of decking that is raised high off the ground, it is best to fit rails on all sides.

You will need

Tools

✔ Pencil, ruler, tape measure, square
✔ Two portable workbenches
✔ Crosscut saw
✔ Cordless electric drill with a cross-point screwdriver bit
✔ Drill bits to match the sizes of the screws and bolts
✔ Ratchet wrench and spirit level
✔ Electric sander

Materials

(All rough-sawn pine includes excess length for wastage. All wood is pressure-treated with preservative.)

For a bench with sides 1.65 m long; rails 2.122 m long, 941 mm high

✔ Pine: 3 rough-sawn pieces, 2 m long, 75 mm square section (posts and bench legs)
✔ Pine: 26 rough-sawn pieces, 2 m long, 40 mm wide and 20 mm thick (balusters and baluster rails)
✔ Pine: 7 rough-sawn pieces, 3 m long, 100 mm wide and 20 mm thick (rails, seat boards, fascia)
✔ Pine: 1 rough-sawn piece, 3 m long, 80 mm wide and 35 mm thick (under-seat stretcher)
✔ Zinc-plated, countersunk cross-headed screws. 50 x 90 mm no. 10, 100 x 35 mm no. 8
✔ Coach bolts: 12 x 150 mm long, with nuts and washers to fit

Overall dimensions and general notes

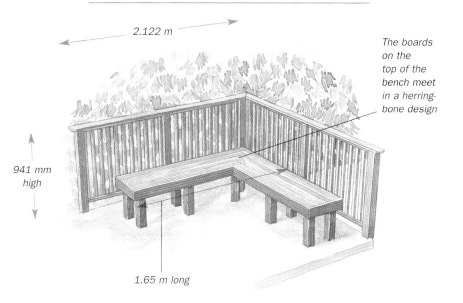

2.122 m

941 mm high

1.65 m long

The boards on the top of the bench meet in a herringbone design

This bench and safety rail combination is suitable for adding to a wide range of decking patios, and is simple to build. It makes a safe place for all the family to relax.

Exploded view of the bench seat and safety rail

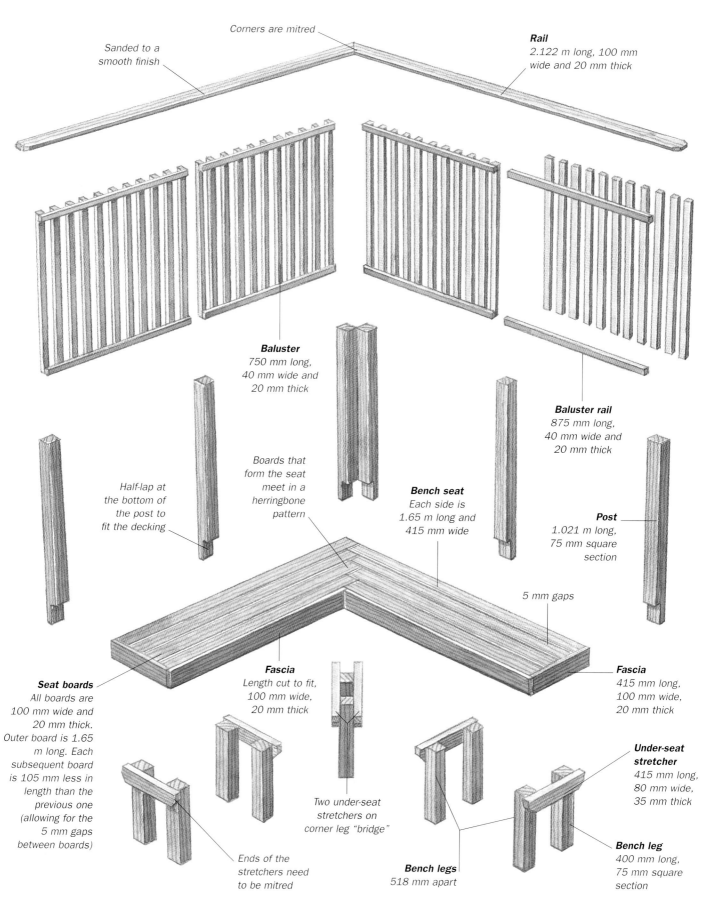

Sanded to a smooth finish

Corners are mitred

Rail
2.122 m long, 100 mm wide and 20 mm thick

Baluster
750 mm long, 40 mm wide and 20 mm thick

Baluster rail
875 mm long, 40 mm wide and 20 mm thick

Half-lap at the bottom of the post to fit the decking

Boards that form the seat meet in a herringbone pattern

Bench seat
Each side is 1.65 m long and 415 mm wide

Post
1.021 m long, 75 mm square section

5 mm gaps

Fascia
Length cut to fit, 100 mm wide, 20 mm thick

Fascia
415 mm long, 100 mm wide, 20 mm thick

Seat boards
All boards are 100 mm wide and 20 mm thick. Outer board is 1.65 m long. Each subsequent board is 105 mm less in length than the previous one (allowing for the 5 mm gaps between boards)

Under-seat stretcher
415 mm long, 80 mm wide, 35 mm thick

Two under-seat stretchers on corner leg "bridge"

Ends of the stretchers need to be mitred

Bench legs
518 mm apart

Bench leg
400 mm long, 75 mm square section

Making the bench seat and safety rail

1 Cutting the posts
Cut the six posts for the uprights of the safety rail assembly to length, cutting half-laps on one end to fit the ring joist (outer frame) of the existing decking. Set the posts in position.

2 Fixing the posts and rails
Fix the posts to the decking joists using 90 mm screws and 150 mm coach bolts. Use the spirit level to ensure that the posts are upright. Cut the two rails to length, complete with a 45° mitre at the corner, and screw them to the top of the posts with 90 mm screws.

3 Building the balusters
With the baluster rails and balusters, build four frames. Set them in place between the posts, and screw them in position. Run screws down through the rails and into the top of the baluster frames. Use 90 mm screws throughout.

4 Making the bench legs
Build the five "bridge" frames that make the legs of the bench – the four frames for the straight sides, and the double-top frame for the corner of the bench. Use 90 mm screws throughout.

5 Fixing the bench legs and seat
Set the leg "bridge" frames in place on the decking and link them with the seat boards, using 35 mm screws. Note the way the boards are cut and fixed in a herringbone pattern at the corner.

6 Making a fascia
Cap the front edges and ends of the bench with a fascia that runs flush to the surface of the bench. Use 35 mm screws throughout. Finally, sand everything to a good finish.

Tree ring seat

When I was a child I used to love sitting on an old ring seat under an apple tree in my grandparents' orchard. I can picture the scene now – the trunk of the old tree to my back, a dappled canopy of leaves overhead, and long, lush grass underfoot. If you have a suitable small tree, this seat will come into its own in summer when you can use it to relax under the leafy shade. Remember to allow room for the trunk to grow.

★ ★ ★
Advanced

Making time
One weekend
*One day for making the
parts and one day for
assembling the seat
around the tree*

Considering the design

The seat is based on a hexagon and built in easy-to-make sections. The idea is that the sections can be prepared in a convenient location – perhaps in the workshop or the garage – and then put together around your chosen tree.

The seat stands about 420 mm above ground level. The legs are built from 50 mm-wide, 32 mm-thick sections, and each pair of legs is bridged with top stretchers. These leg units are in turn joined to each other with linking stretchers, making the hexagonal design seen in plan view. The construction is topped with a seat made from 94 mm-wide grooved decking boards, and the front edge of the seat is trimmed with a decorative wavy frieze or apron.

Getting started

Search out an appropriate tree, and decide whether or not the project needs to be modified according to the dimensions of the trunk. Cut all the wood to length, tidy up the sawn ends with sandpaper, and stack it in readiness. Set out the two workbenches in your chosen working area and generally arrange your tools for the task ahead.

You will need

Tools

- ✔ Pencil, ruler, tape measure, square and tracing paper
- ✔ Two portable workbenches
- ✔ Crosscut saw
- ✔ Cordless electric drill
- ✔ Drill bits to match the screw size
- ✔ Hand cross-point screwdriver
- ✔ Electric jigsaw and electric sander
- ✔ Pair of clamps

Materials

(All rough-sawn pine includes excess length for wastage. All the wood is pressure-treated with preservative.)

For a seat 1.285 m in diameter

- ✔ Pine: 2 rough-sawn pieces, 3 m long, 50 mm wide and 32 mm thick (legs)
- ✔ Pine: 2 rough-sawn pieces, 3 m long, 75 mm wide and 20 mm thick (top stretchers)
- ✔ Pine: 2 rough-sawn pieces, 3 m long, 50 mm wide and 37 mm thick (linking stretchers)
- ✔ Pine: 2 pieces planed and grooved decking, 3 m long, 94 mm wide, 20 mm thick (decorative frieze)
- ✔ Pine: 3 pieces planed and grooved decking, 3 m long, 94 mm wide and 20 mm thick (seating boards)
- ✔ Zinc-plated, countersunk cross-headed screws: 200 x 55 mm no. 8

Overall dimensions and general notes

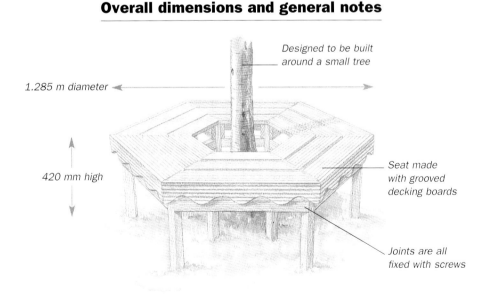

1.285 m diameter

420 mm high

Designed to be built around a small tree

Seat made with grooved decking boards

Joints are all fixed with screws

This is a traditional design for freestanding seating to fit around a tree, and it works best on a level site. It could be used to complement the Patio with Sandpit on page 76.

Exploded view of the tree ring seat

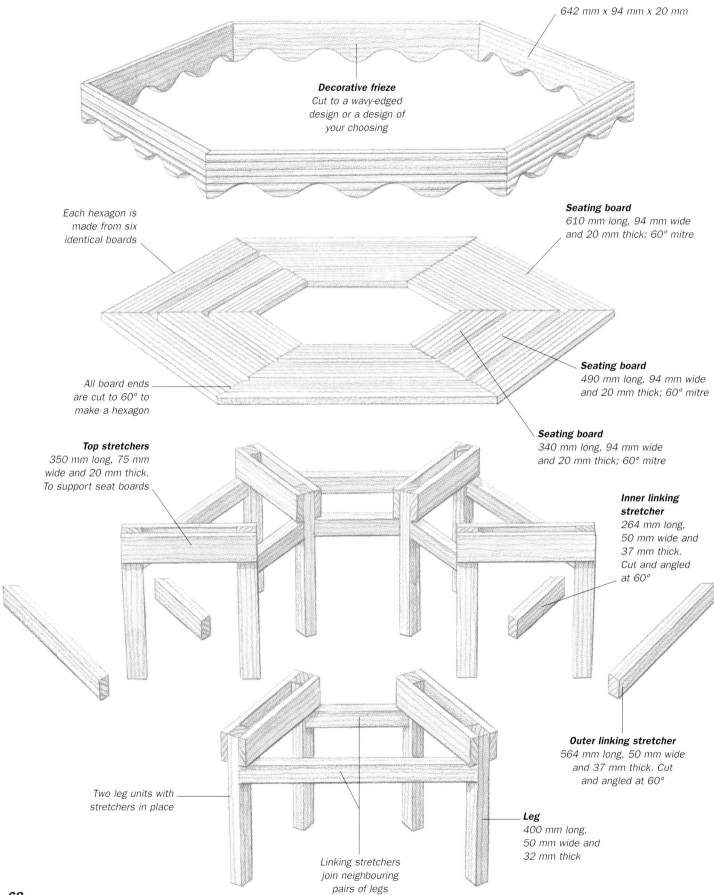

642 mm x 94 mm x 20 mm

Decorative frieze
Cut to a wavy-edged design or a design of your choosing

Each hexagon is made from six identical boards

Seating board
610 mm long, 94 mm wide and 20 mm thick; 60° mitre

All board ends are cut to 60° to make a hexagon

Seating board
490 mm long, 94 mm wide and 20 mm thick; 60° mitre

Seating board
340 mm long, 94 mm wide and 20 mm thick; 60° mitre

Top stretchers
350 mm long, 75 mm wide and 20 mm thick. To support seat boards

Inner linking stretcher
264 mm long, 50 mm wide and 37 mm thick. Cut and angled at 60°

Two leg units with stretchers in place

Outer linking stretcher
564 mm long, 50 mm wide and 37 mm thick. Cut and angled at 60°

Leg
400 mm long, 50 mm wide and 32 mm thick

Linking stretchers join neighbouring pairs of legs

Making the tree ring seat

1 Making the leg units
Sandwich two legs between two top stretchers, so that you have a frame 400 mm high and 350 mm wide. Fix each end of each stretcher to the leg with two screws, with the screws offset (see photo). Build six such frames.

2 Fixing the stretchers
When you have made all six leg units, take the inner and outer linking stretchers (all cut to length and angled at 60°) and screw the units together in pairs. You should finish up with three identical angle-ended bench units.

3 Joining the structure
Set the three identical bench units around your chosen tree, spacing them to make a hexagon. Screw the remaining linking stretchers in place to join neighbouring bench units.

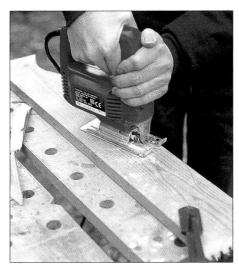

4 Fitting the seat
Take the seating boards (three different lengths for each of the six sections) and screw them on top of the frame. Make sure that the sawn ends are centred on the leg frames.

5 Making the decorative frieze
Draw the wavy design on tracing paper and with a pencil, press-transfer the drawn lines through to the 94 mm-wide frieze boards. Cut out the design with the jigsaw and use the sander to tidy up the sawn edges.

6 Finishing
Finally, clamp and screw the frieze boards around the seat so that the top edge is flush with the top of the seat. Use the sander to rub down the whole seat area to a smooth finish.

Adirondack chair

★ ★ ★
Advanced

This beautiful folk art chair gets its name from the Adirondack Mountains in north-east New York State in America, where, in the middle of the nineteenth century, chairs of this type were first made. It is characterized by the flowing shape of the side boards, the roll of the seat, the fan back and the broad, flat arms. These chairs were originally made from scrap such as crates, salvaged wood, or waste from sawmills.

Making time
One weekend
One day for building the basic chair, and one day for finishing

Considering the design

We have modified the basic Adirondack chair design by hinging the arms to the front legs and the seat back, and by fixing a swivel pin between the arms and the fretted side boards so that the chair can be packed flat for winter storage. The design uses only rough-sawn wood, and cutting has been kept to the minimum.

Getting started

Note the various lengths and sections in the working drawings, and then saw your wood to size. Stack the wood in four groups: for the basic seat unit, the front legs and arms, the seat back, and the little pieces needed under the seat.

Overall dimensions and general notes

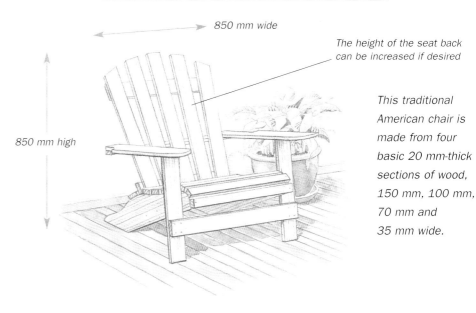

850 mm wide

850 mm high

The height of the seat back can be increased if desired

This traditional American chair is made from four basic 20 mm-thick sections of wood, 150 mm, 100 mm, 70 mm and 35 mm wide.

You will need

Tools

- ✔ Pencil, ruler, tape measure, compass and square
- ✔ Two portable workbenches
- ✔ Crosscut saw
- ✔ Electric jigsaw
- ✔ Cordless electric drill with a cross-point screwdriver bit
- ✔ Drill bits to match the sizes of the screws
- ✔ Electric sander
- ✔ Paintbrush

Materials

(All rough-sawn pieces of pine include excess length for wastage. All the wood is pressure-treated with preservative.)

For one chair, 850 mm wide and 850 mm high

- ✔ Pine: 2 rough-sawn pieces, 2 m long, 150 mm wide and 20 mm thick (side and arm boards)
- ✔ Pine: 3 rough-sawn pieces, 2 m long, 100 mm wide and 20 mm thick (front legs, stretcher board, stop boards)
- ✔ Pine: 6 rough-sawn pieces, 2 m long, 70 mm wide and 20 mm thick (seat back, back supports, fan support bar and wide seat boards)

- ✔ Pine: 1 rough-sawn piece, 2 m long, 35 mm wide and 20 mm thick (narrow seat boards)
- ✔ Pine: 1 rough-sawn piece, 1 m long, 35 mm square (under-seat fixing blocks)
- ✔ Zinc-plated, countersunk cross-headed screws: 100 x 35 mm no. 8, quantity of 15 mm no. 8 (number to fit your chosen hinges), 2 x 100 mm no. 10 (with washers to fit)
- ✔ Hinges: 4 painted 200 mm-long T-hinges (the type used for gates)
- ✔ Exterior-grade white masonry paint in a matt finish
- ✔ Danish oil

Perspective view of the Adirondack chair

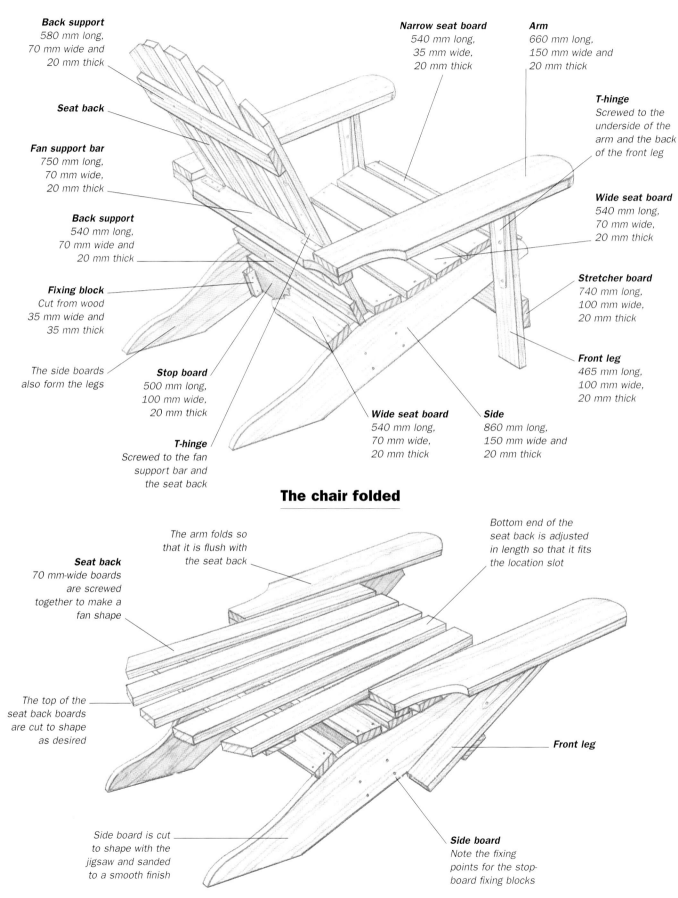

Back support
*580 mm long,
70 mm wide and
20 mm thick*

Seat back

Fan support bar
*750 mm long,
70 mm wide,
20 mm thick*

Back support
*540 mm long,
70 mm wide and
20 mm thick*

Fixing block
*Cut from wood
35 mm wide and
35 mm thick*

*The side boards
also form the legs*

Stop board
*500 mm long,
100 mm wide,
20 mm thick*

T-hinge
*Screwed to the fan
support bar and
the seat back*

Narrow seat board
*540 mm long,
35 mm wide,
20 mm thick*

Arm
*660 mm long,
150 mm wide and
20 mm thick*

T-hinge
*Screwed to the
underside of the
arm and the back
of the front leg*

Wide seat board
*540 mm long,
70 mm wide,
20 mm thick*

Stretcher board
*740 mm long,
100 mm wide,
20 mm thick*

Front leg
*465 mm long,
100 mm wide,
20 mm thick*

Wide seat board
*540 mm long,
70 mm wide,
20 mm thick*

Side
*860 mm long,
150 mm wide and
20 mm thick*

The chair folded

Seat back
*70 mm-wide boards
are screwed
together to make a
fan shape*

*The arm folds so
that it is flush with
the seat back*

*Bottom end of the
seat back is adjusted
in length so that it fits
the location slot*

*The top of the
seat back boards
are cut to shape
as desired*

*Side board is cut
to shape with the
jigsaw and sanded
to a smooth finish*

Front leg

Side board
*Note the fixing
points for the stop-
board fixing blocks*

The chair components

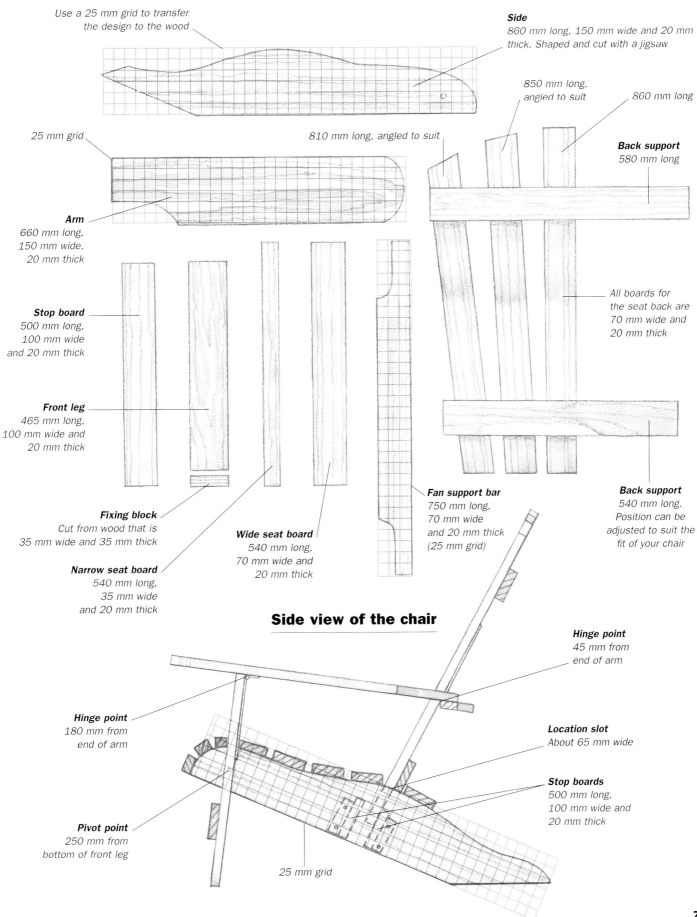

Use a 25 mm grid to transfer the design to the wood

Side
860 mm long, 150 mm wide and 20 mm thick. Shaped and cut with a jigsaw

850 mm long, angled to suit

860 mm long

25 mm grid

810 mm long, angled to suit

Back support
580 mm long

Arm
660 mm long,
150 mm wide,
20 mm thick

All boards for
the seat back are
70 mm wide and
20 mm thick

Stop board
500 mm long,
100 mm wide
and 20 mm thick

Front leg
465 mm long,
100 mm wide and
20 mm thick

Fixing block
Cut from wood that is
35 mm wide and 35 mm thick

Fan support bar
750 mm long,
70 mm wide
and 20 mm thick
(25 mm grid)

Back support
540 mm long.
Position can be
adjusted to suit the
fit of your chair

Wide seat board
540 mm long,
70 mm wide and
20 mm thick

Narrow seat board
540 mm long,
35 mm wide
and 20 mm thick

Side view of the chair

Hinge point
45 mm from
end of arm

Hinge point
180 mm from
end of arm

Location slot
About 65 mm wide

Stop boards
500 mm long,
100 mm wide and
20 mm thick

Pivot point
250 mm from
bottom of front leg

25 mm grid

73

Making the Adirondack chair

1 Cutting the boards
Draw curves on the appropriate boards for the two arms, the two side boards, the five seat back boards, and the single fan support bar that links the ends of the arms across the chair back. Use the jigsaw to fret out the shapes.

2 Making the seat
To form the seat, take three narrow seat boards and four wide seat boards, and screw them to the two side boards with 35 mm screws. (A final wide seat board is added later.) The two sides must be parallel to each other and square with the seat.

3 Making the legs
Take the two boards that make the front legs, link them with the stretcher board – to make the characteristic H-frame – and fix them with four 35 mm screws at each intersection.

4 Hinging the arms
Set the two arms face down, and hinge them to the front H-frame. Note that the stretcher board is placed so that it lies across the front of the legs.

5 Attaching the fan support
Screw the fan support bar to the back ends of the two arm boards, all the while making sure that all the components are square to each other.

6 Pivoting the seat

Drill pivot holes through the side boards. Slide the washers on the 100 mm screws and run the screws through the side board holes and on into the thickness of the front legs.

7 Making the location slot

Position the chair so that the top of the seat is uppermost, and screw the eighth seat board in place with 35 mm screws. Leave a 65 mm gap between the eighth board and the one before it to make the location slot for the seat back.

8 Fixing the stop boards

With the underside of the seat uppermost, fix the two stop boards (to secure the seat back in the location slot) in place with 35 mm screws and the under-seat fixing blocks. Screw the blocks to the stop boards first, then screw the blocks to the side boards.

9 Making the back

Take the five seat back boards, and place them best face down, arranging them into a fan shape. Spread of fan at position of bottom edge of back support bar must not exceed 500 mm. Screw the two back supports in place with 35 mm screws.

10 Fixing the back

Slide the seat back into the location slot, raise the arms up so that it is supported, and hinge the seat back to the fan support bar with 15 mm screws. Paint the chair, let it dry, rub it down so that it looks worn at the edges and ends, and then give it a coat of Danish oil.

Patio with sandpit

★ ★ ★
Advanced

Picture this... the sun is shining, you are relaxed and stretched out on wooden decking, there is a dappled canopy of leaves overhead, and there is a child at your side happily playing in a sandpit. If you choose this project, that scene could become reality after a weekend's work. The structure measures 2.9 m long by 2 m wide, but there is no reason why you cannot make it bigger or smaller to suit your garden situation.

Making time
One weekend
One day for the basic structure, and one day for fixing the decking and finishing

Considering the design

There are holes to accommodate the sandpit and a tree. The decking boards are slightly cut back around the sandpit, so that the resultant board-thickness step between the surface of the decking and the top face of the beam becomes the lip for the pet-proof hatch cover. Because children will be crawling over the decking, make sure that a sealant is used over the preserved wood.

Getting started

Look at your site and choose a level area with a suitable tree. Measure the girth of the tree, and decide just where the sandpit will be placed. Choose your wood with extra care, and make sure that it is free from loose knots and splits.

Overall dimensions and general notes

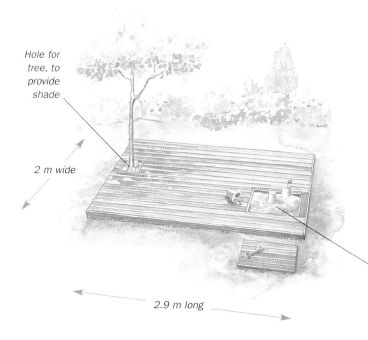

Hole for tree, to provide shade

2 m wide

2.9 m long

The patio consists of decking boards (100 mm wide and 20 mm thick) supported by joists (100 mm square section). The joists are 400 mm apart at their centres.

The sandpit has a cover to keep the sand clean

You will need

Tools

✔ Pencil, ruler, tape measure and square
✔ Pegs and string
✔ Two portable workbenches
✔ Crosscut saw
✔ Cordless electric drill with a cross-point screwdriver bit
✔ Drill bit to match the size of the screws
✔ Claw hammer
✔ Electric sander
✔ Paintbrush

Materials

(All rough-sawn pieces of pine include excess length for wastage. All the wood is pressure-treated with preservative)

For a patio 2.9 m long and 2 m wide

✔ Pine: 8 rough-sawn pieces, 2 m long, 100 mm square section (joists)
✔ Pine: 22 rough-sawn pieces, 3 m long, 100 mm wide and 20 mm thick (decking boards, frames and fascias)
✔ Pine: 1 rough-sawn piece, 2 m long, 40 mm wide and 20 mm thick (sandpit hatch cover battens)
✔ Woven plastic sheet: 3 m long and 2 m wide (to go under the decking)
✔ Nails: 1 kg of 125 mm x 5.6 mm
✔ Zinc-plated, countersunk cross-headed screws: 300 x 50 mm no. 8, 50 x 35 mm no.8
✔ Matt decking sealant
✔ Soft sand: 50 kg washed soft sand

Exploded view of the patio with sandpit

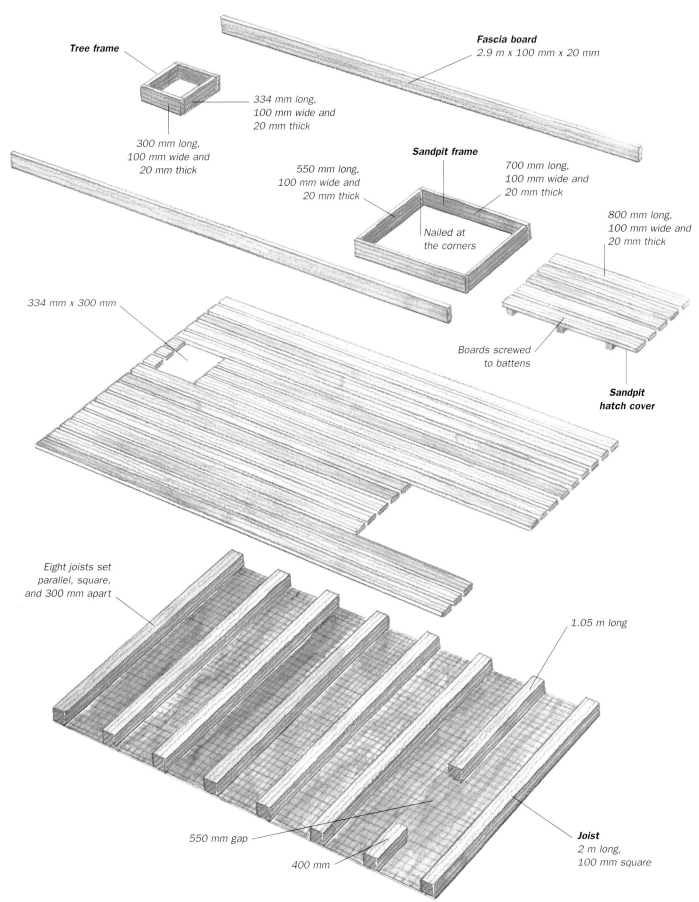

Tree frame

Fascia board
2.9 m x 100 mm x 20 mm

334 mm long,
100 mm wide and
20 mm thick

300 mm long,
100 mm wide and
20 mm thick

550 mm long,
100 mm wide and
20 mm thick

Sandpit frame

700 mm long,
100 mm wide and
20 mm thick

Nailed at
the corners

800 mm long,
100 mm wide and
20 mm thick

334 mm x 300 mm

Boards screwed
to battens

**Sandpit
hatch cover**

Eight joists set
parallel, square,
and 300 mm apart

1.05 m long

550 mm gap

400 mm

Joist
2 m long,
100 mm square

Exploded view of the patio with sandpit

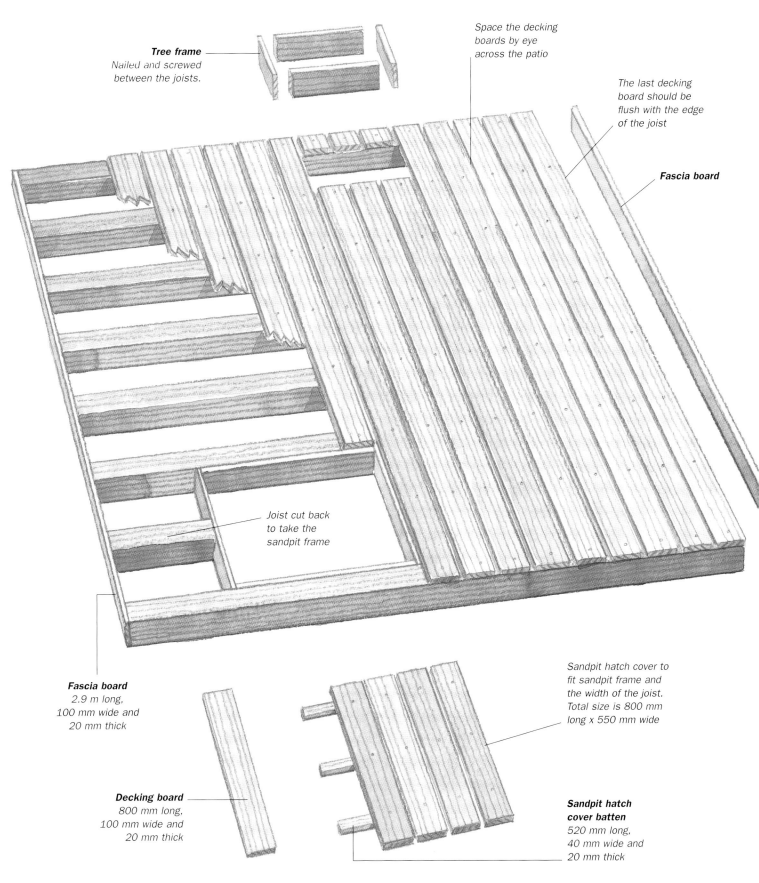

Tree frame
*Nailed and screwed
between the joists.*

*Space the decking
boards by eye
across the patio*

*The last decking
board should be
flush with the edge
of the joist*

Fascia board

*Joist cut back
to take the
sandpit frame*

Fascia board
*2.9 m long,
100 mm wide and
20 mm thick*

Decking board
*800 mm long,
100 mm wide and
20 mm thick*

*Sandpit hatch cover to
fit sandpit frame and
the width of the joist.
Total size is 800 mm
long x 550 mm wide*

**Sandpit hatch
cover batten**
*520 mm long,
40 mm wide and
20 mm thick*

Making the patio with sandpit

1 Cutting the joists

Cut the joists to length (allowing for the sandpit area) and set them in position on the site, together with a couple of decking boards, to give you an idea of how the finished project will look. Decide exactly where they will lie in relation to the tree.

2 Fixing the joists

Cover the whole site with the woven plastic sheeting, leaving a hole around the tree. Position the joists, setting them square with the plastic and parallel to each other. Fix them in place with a decking board at each side, using one screw at each intersection.

3 Squaring the frame

To ensure that the frame is square, measure the diagonals and make adjustments to the frame until both diagonals are equal. Drive in a second screw at each corner.

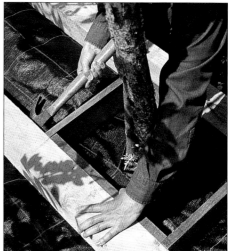

4 Making the frames

Build two frames – a tree frame to go around the tree, and a sandpit frame for the sandpit. Nail and screw the frames in place between the joists.

5 Fixing the decking

Cut and fit all the long decking boards, which run the full length of the frame. Screw them to the joists. Set them flush with the sides of the two frames. Leave a 550 mm gap between the boards for the sandpit, and a 334 mm gap for the tree.

6 Completing the decking

Cut and fit all the other shorter decking boards, spacing them as before. They should be stepped back around the sandpit frame to provide a lip for the sandpit hatch cover, and flush with the tree frame. Cut boards for the sandpit hatch cover.

7 Fixing the fascia boards

Fit the fascia boards along the two long sides of the decking, covering the ends of the joists. Position the edges of the boards so that they are flush with the surface of the decking.

8 Making the sandpit hatch cover

Fix the boards for the sandpit hatch cover to the three battens. Space them to match the rest of the decking. Finally, rub down the structure with the sander, give all the surfaces two or three coats of matt sealant and fill the sandpit.

Hillside decking

This decking is designed specifically to be built on a piece of gently sloping ground. You simply cut the posts to length to suit the slope, and then bolt them to the platform and set them in concrete. Working in this way, it is easy to adapt the structure to suit just about any situation. The project is made up from three basic platforms: one set at ground level, one set higher up the slope, and a mini platform that is used as a step.

★ ★ ★
Advanced

Making time
One long weekend
One day for the basic frames and one day for fixing and fitting the posts, and finishing

Considering the design

The joists are butted and screwed at the corners, and then bolted to the posts. The upper platform has been set at a 45° angle to the lower one. The three platforms are built as separate units, which allows you to change things around to suit the slope and layout of your garden.

Getting started

Work out how you want the platforms to be positioned in relation to each other. If you find it difficult to picture, build the lower one and set it in the ground, then build the upper one and move it around until you find a suitable position.

Overall dimensions and general notes

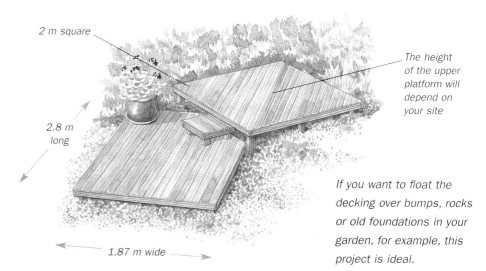

2 m square

2.8 m long

1.87 m wide

The height of the upper platform will depend on your site

If you want to float the decking over bumps, rocks or old foundations in your garden, for example, this project is ideal.

You will need

Tools

- ✔ Pencil, ruler, tape measure and square
- ✔ Two portable workbenches
- ✔ Crosscut saw
- ✔ Cordless electric drill with a cross-point screwdriver bit
- ✔ Drill bits to match the sizes of the screws and bolts
- ✔ Spade
- ✔ Wrench to fit the bolts
- ✔ Wheelbarrow
- ✔ Bucket
- ✔ Shovel and pointing trowel

- ✔ Spirit level
- ✔ Sledgehammer
- ✔ Electric sander

Materials

(All rough-sawn pieces of pine include excess length for wastage. All the wood is pressure-treated with preservative.)

For two areas of decking: 2.8 m x 1.87 m, and 2 m square

- ✔ Pine: 5 rough-sawn pieces, 2 m long, 75 mm square section (posts)
- ✔ Pine: 22 rough-sawn pieces, 2 m long, 85 mm wide and 40 mm thick; 2 pieces, 3 m long, 85 mm wide

and 40 mm thick (joists, frames and noggings)

- ✔ Pine: 34 rough-sawn pieces, 3 m long, 100 mm wide and 20 mm thick (decking boards)
- ✔ Pine: 2 rough-sawn pieces, 3 m long, 35 mm wide and 20 mm thick (temporary battens)
- ✔ Zinc-plated, countersunk cross-headed screws: 300 x 40 mm no. 8, 100 x 90 mm no. 10
- ✔ Zinc plated coach bolts with nuts and washers to fit: 30 x 150 mm
- ✔ Concrete: 1 part (50 kg) cement, 2 parts (100 kg) sharp sand, 3 parts (150 kg) aggregate

Exploded view of the hillside decking

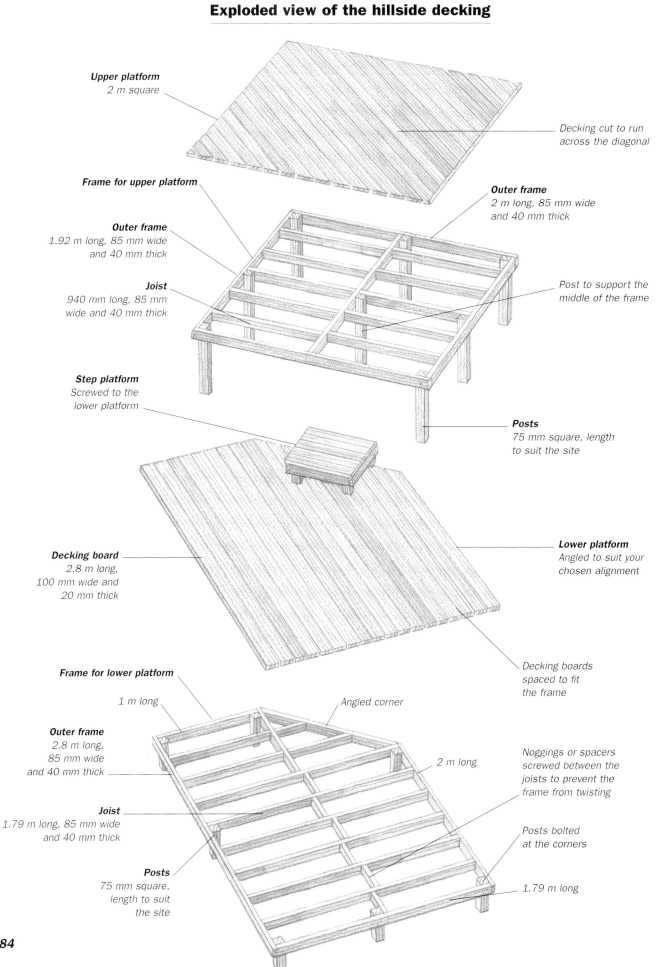

Upper platform
2 m square

Decking cut to run
across the diagonal

Frame for upper platform

Outer frame
2 m long, 85 mm wide
and 40 mm thick

Outer frame
1.92 m long, 85 mm wide
and 40 mm thick

Joist
940 mm long, 85 mm
wide and 40 mm thick

Post to support the
middle of the frame

Step platform
Screwed to the
lower platform

Posts
75 mm square, length
to suit the site

Decking board
2.8 m long,
100 mm wide and
20 mm thick

Lower platform
Angled to suit your
chosen alignment

Decking boards
spaced to fit
the frame

Frame for lower platform

1 m long

Angled corner

Outer frame
2.8 m long,
85 mm wide
and 40 mm thick

2 m long

Noggings or spacers
screwed between the
joists to prevent the
frame from twisting

Joist
1.79 m long, 85 mm wide
and 40 mm thick

Posts bolted
at the corners

Posts
75 mm square,
length to suit
the site

1.79 m long

Plan view of the hillside decking

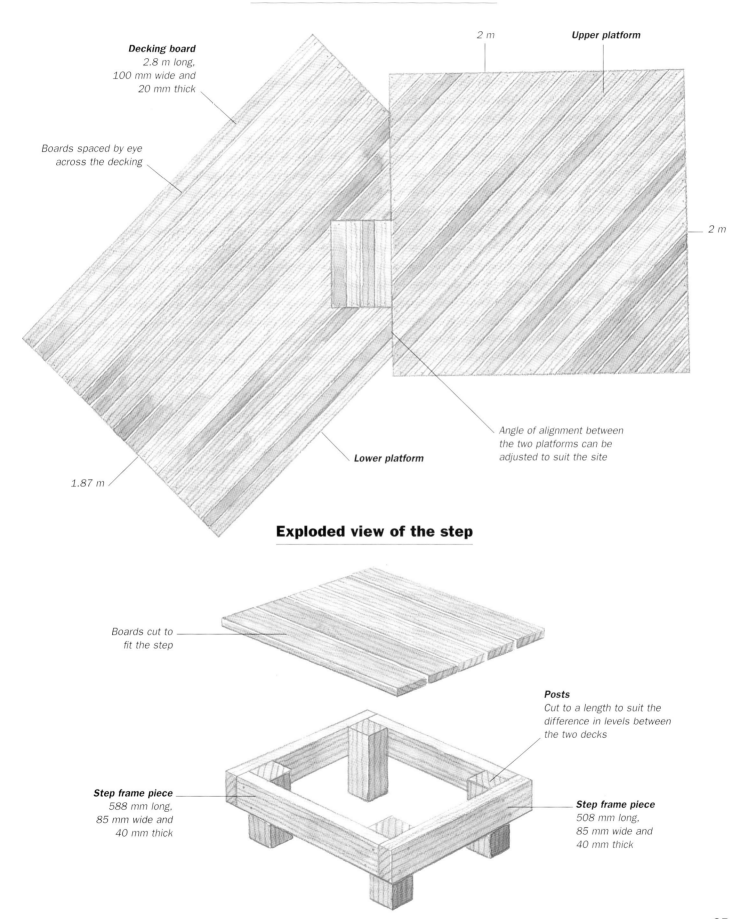

Decking board
2.8 m long,
100 mm wide and
20 mm thick

Boards spaced by eye
across the decking

2 m

Upper platform

2 m

Angle of alignment between
the two platforms can be
adjusted to suit the site

Lower platform

1.87 m

Exploded view of the step

Boards cut to
fit the step

Posts
Cut to a length to suit the
difference in levels between
the two decks

Step frame piece
588 mm long,
85 mm wide and
40 mm thick

Step frame piece
508 mm long,
85 mm wide and
40 mm thick

Making the hillside decking

1 Planning
Use the joists to plan out the total design on the ground. Work out the precise dimensions of the lower platform and the position of the post holes.

2 Lower platform frame
Cut the wood for the outer frame, butt the pieces at the corners and fix with 90 mm screws. Cut the diagonal piece for the angled corner to suit the frame. Fit in place. With 40 mm screws, screw temporary battens across the diagonals to hold the frame square.

3 Fitting the joists
Cut the joists and place them inside the outer frame so that they are set a little over 300 mm apart at their centres. Fix each joint with two 90 mm screws.

4 Digging the post holes
Set the frame level on the ground and establish the position of the posts within the frame. Dig a 300 mm-deep hole for each post. Set the posts in place and trim them to length to suit the height of the frame off the ground.

5 Attaching the posts
Bolt the posts to the frame, so that the tops are just level with the top of the frame. Repeat all the procedures just described to make the upper platform, and then set it in place.

6 Checking levels

Check each frame with the spirit level to make sure that it is horizontal, and make any small adjustments either by using the sledgehammer to tap down the posts, or by wedging the frames with offcuts.

7 Concreting the posts

Set both frames in their post holes. Mix a stiff batch of concrete and tamp it into the holes around the posts, filling them almost up to ground level. Trowel the concrete flush with the ground and shape it so that rainwater will flow away from the posts.

8 Fixing the decking

Screw the decking boards across the upper platform frame with 40 mm screws, so that they are at 45° to the sides. Use the crosscut saw to trim the waste ends so that the edge runs parallel to the frame. Fix decking boards to the lower platform.

9 Building the step

Repeat the procedures in Steps 1–8 to build a small platform to act as a step (modify to suit your decking). Screw the step to the lower platform with 90 mm screws, running the screws down through the legs at a sharp angle. Finally, sand everything to a good finish.

Waterside raised decking

Raised decking is a wonderfully exciting feature for a garden that backs on to a stretch of water. It's a magical feeling to be raised up high and looking out over a lake, river or the sea. This project is time-consuming and a challenge, but the design is easy to understand. The order of work is to first set the posts in concrete, then bolt a frame to the posts to establish the level of the decking, and fill in the frame with joists.

Making time
Two weekends
One weekend for the basic frame; second weekend for the balusters and details

Considering the design

Decking is laid over the joists, the posts are trimmed to establish the level of the handrail, then the balusters are made.

Getting started

Only six of the ten posts are set in the ground, but in your particular situation this may vary: study your site, decide where the decking is going, and see how many posts need to be set in concrete.

Overall dimensions and general notes

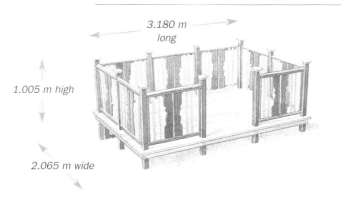

3.180 m long

1.005 m high

2.065 m wide

This decking is designed to be built on a riverbank, or could overhang a pond. You can choose where the baluster rail panels go – the entrance can be moved.

You will need

Tools

(Warning. Because you are working by water, mains power tools must be used in conjunction with an electricity circuit breaker.)

- ✔ Pencil, ruler, tape measure and square
- ✔ Two portable workbenches
- ✔ Crosscut saw
- ✔ Spade and shovel
- ✔ Wrench to fit your chosen nuts
- ✔ Sledgehammer
- ✔ Spirit level
- ✔ Cordless electric drill with a cross-point screwdriver bit
- ✔ Drill bits to match the sizes of the screws and bolts
- ✔ Wheelbarrow, bucket and trowel
- ✔ Electric jigsaw
- ✔ Pair of clamps
- ✔ Electric sander

Materials

(All rough-sawn pieces of pine include excess length for wastage and design modifications. All the wood is pressure-treated with preservative.)

For raised decking 3.180 m long, 2.065 m wide, and 1.005 m high

- ✔ Pine: 14 rough-sawn pieces, 3 m long, 75 mm square section (ten main posts and secondary posts, joist supports, bracing beams)
- ✔ Pine: 15 rough-sawn pieces, 3 m long, 87 mm wide and 40 mm thick (joists, noggings, temporary battens)
- ✔ Pine: 27 pieces planed and grooved decking board, 3 m long, 120 mm wide and 30 mm thick (floor and any steps that might be needed)

- ✔ Pine: 15 rough-sawn pieces 3 m long, 50 mm wide and 30 mm thick (baluster rails and fixing battens)
- ✔ Pine: 4 rough-sawn pieces, 3 m long, 60 mm wide and 30 mm thick (pitch-topped rail capping)
- ✔ Pine: 15 rough-sawn pieces, 2 m long, 40 mm wide and 20 mm thick (slender balusters or vertical rails)
- ✔ Pine: 12 rough-sawn pieces, 3 m long, 150 mm wide and 20 mm thick (wide fretted baluster boards and newel post caps)
- ✔ Zinc-plated coach bolts with washers and nuts to fit: 36 x 120 mm, 16 x 180 mm
- ✔ Zinc-plated, countersunk cross-headed screws: 400 x 90 mm no. 8, 400 x 75 mm no. 10
- ✔ Concrete: 1 part (50 kg) cement, 2 parts (100 kg) sharp sand, 3 parts (150 kg) aggregate
- ✔ Hardcore: 1 bucket for each post

Exploded view of the waterside raised decking

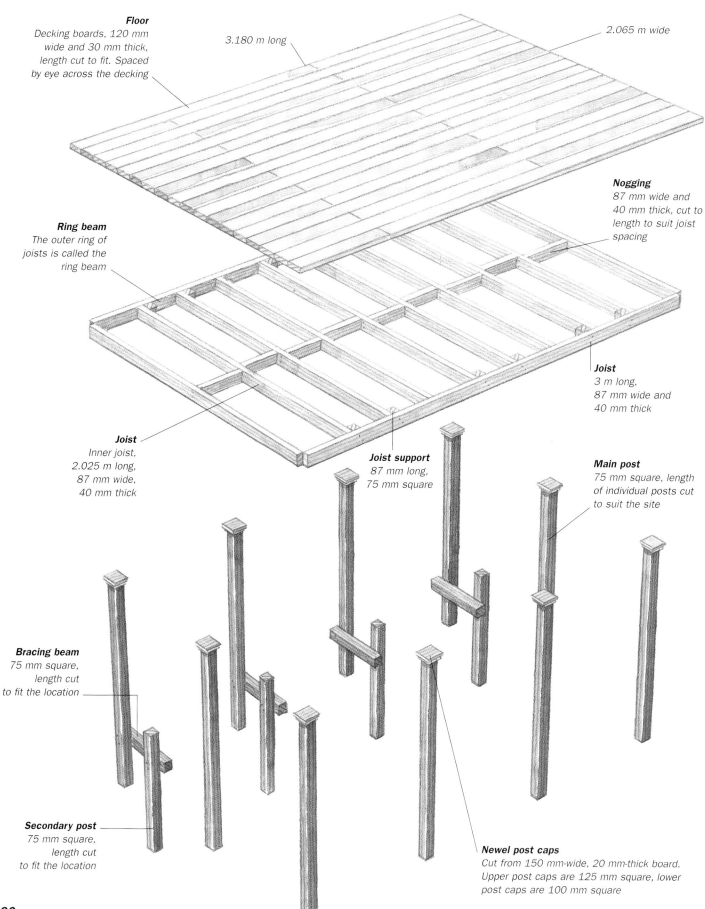

Floor
Decking boards, 120 mm wide and 30 mm thick, length cut to fit. Spaced by eye across the decking

3.180 m long

2.065 m wide

Nogging
87 mm wide and 40 mm thick, cut to length to suit joist spacing

Ring beam
The outer ring of joists is called the ring beam

Joist
3 m long, 87 mm wide and 40 mm thick

Joist
Inner joist, 2.025 m long, 87 mm wide, 40 mm thick

Joist support
87 mm long, 75 mm square

Main post
75 mm square, length of individual posts cut to suit the site

Bracing beam
75 mm square, length cut to fit the location

Secondary post
75 mm square, length cut to fit the location

Newel post caps
Cut from 150 mm-wide, 20 mm-thick board. Upper post caps are 125 mm square, lower post caps are 100 mm square

Front view of the waterside raised decking (viewed from the water)

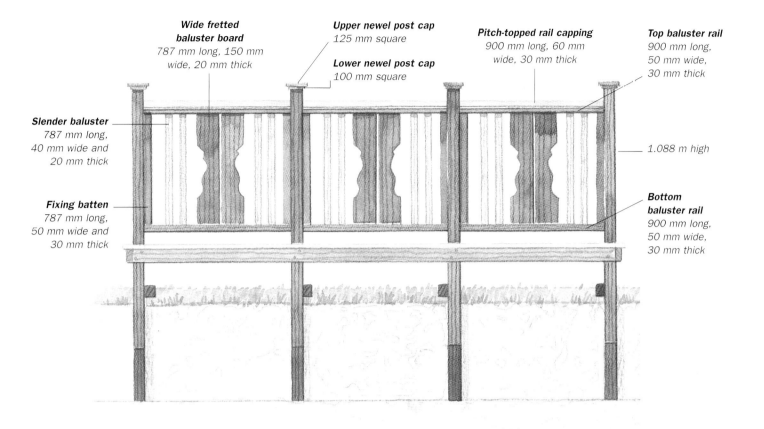

Wide fretted baluster board
787 mm long, 150 mm wide, 20 mm thick

Upper newel post cap
125 mm square

Lower newel post cap
100 mm square

Pitch-topped rail capping
900 mm long, 60 mm wide, 30 mm thick

Top baluster rail
900 mm long, 50 mm wide, 30 mm thick

Slender baluster
787 mm long, 40 mm wide and 20 mm thick

1.088 m high

Fixing batten
787 mm long, 50 mm wide and 30 mm thick

Bottom baluster rail
900 mm long, 50 mm wide, 30 mm thick

Side view of the waterside raised decking

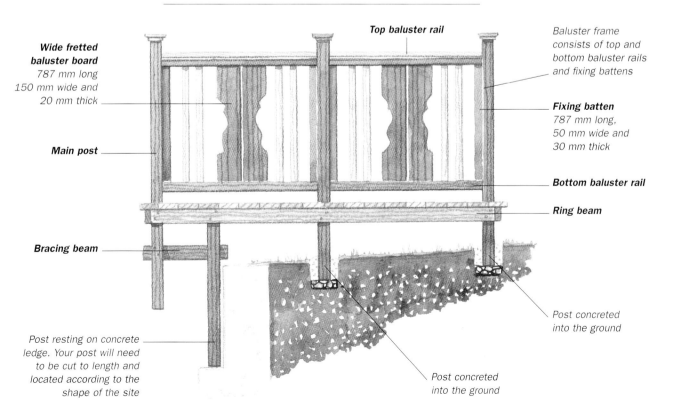

Wide fretted baluster board
787 mm long 150 mm wide and 20 mm thick

Top baluster rail

Baluster frame consists of top and bottom baluster rails and fixing battens

Main post

Fixing batten
787 mm long, 50 mm wide and 30 mm thick

Bottom baluster rail

Ring beam

Bracing beam

Post concreted into the ground

Post resting on concrete ledge. *Your post will need to be cut to length and located according to the shape of the site*

Post concreted into the ground

Making the waterside raised decking

1 Digging post holes

Dig holes for the main posts that require them, to a depth of 300 mm. Set the main posts in them. Loosely bolt the outer ring of joists (ring beam) to the main posts and outer secondary posts to create the frame.

2 Levelling

With the spirit level, check that the ring beam is level. Adjust the height of individual posts if necessary, by standing them on hardcore. (Compact the hardcore with the sledgehammer.) Use the wrench to tightly clench the bolts holding the posts to the ring beam.

3 Concreting the posts

Screw the inner joists in place in the frame with 90 mm screws, complete with noggings and joist supports. Check that the whole structure is square. Make a fairly stiff mix of concrete and pour it into the post holes around the posts. Trowel to a good finish.

4 Fitting the secondary posts

Using coach bolts, fix the secondary posts, bracing beams, and braces. Saw off the secondary posts level with the joists. Saw off the main posts level with each other and screw a temporary batten across the top to hold them square.

6 Cutting the wide balusters
Draw the decorative profile on the 150 mm-wide boards and use the jigsaw to fret out the shape. Rub the sawn edges to a smooth finish.

5 Fixing the floor
Screw the decking boards across the framework of joists with 75 mm screws, making sure that the joints between boards are staggered. Cut and fix the leading boards so that you see a nosing as you approach the decking from the garden.

7 Making the baluster frames
Make up the baluster frames on the ground, complete with fixing battens, top and bottom baluster rails, pitch-topped rail capping, slender balusters and wide fretted balusters. Fix together with 75 mm screws.

8 Finishing
Clamp the baluster frames between the posts and fix them with 90 mm screws. Cut and fix the upper and lower newel post caps to the top of the posts with 75 mm screws. Finally, rub down the whole structure with the sander.

Glossary

Aligning
Setting one component part against another and obtaining a good fit or alignment of the two.

Backfilling
Filling post holes with hardcore and/or concrete in order to stabilize the posts. Also to fill the area surrounding the post to bring it up to the desired level.

Bracing
Minimizing any sideways or skewing movement in a structure by adding a secondary member to triangulate it.

Butting
Pushing one component part hard up against another in order to obtain a good, flush fit, with both faces touching.

Centring
Marking and placing a component in the centre of another. Also measuring from the centre of one component to the centre of another.

Cladding
Covering a frame with decking boards.

Dry run
Putting part of a project together without nails, screws or bolts, in order to see whether or not the components are going to fit, and to make sure that the design is going to work out successfully.

Finishing
The final procedure, at the end of a project, of sanding, painting, staining, oiling or washing down, in order to complete the project.

Framing
Fixing horizontal joists and beams to vertical posts.

Jointing
The procedure of fixing one length of wood to another by means of screws, nails, bolts, or a traditional cut woodworking joint.

Levelling
Using a spirit level to decide whether or not a component part is horizontally parallel to the ground or vertically at right angles to the ground, and then going on to make adjustments to bring the component into line.

Marking out
Variously using a pencil, rule, square, compass, pegs and string to draw lines on a piece of wood, or mark out an area on the ground, in readiness for cutting or otherwise taking a project forward.

Planning and designing
The whole procedure of considering a project, looking at the materials, making drawings, and working out amounts and costs, prior to actually starting work.

Sawing to size
Taking sawn wood (meaning wood that has been purchased ready sawn to width and thickness) and cutting it to length.

Sighting
To judge by eye, or to look down a tool, or down a length of wood, in order to determine whether or not a cut, joint or structure is level or true.

Siting
The act of walking around the garden and taking everything into consideration in order to decide whereabouts a project is going to be placed.

Sourcing
The process of questioning suppliers by phone, visit, letter or e-mail, in order to ascertain the best source for materials.

Squaring
The technique of marking out, with a set square and/or spirit level, to make sure that one surface or structure is at right angles to another.

Squaring a frame
Ensuring squareness (90° corners) in a rectilinear frame by measuring across the diagonals and making adjustments until both diagonals are identical – at which point the frame is square.

Trimming
The act of bringing wood to a good finish with sandpaper and paint. Also a technique for preventing a frame from becoming skewed, by adding noggings or trimming pieces.

Suppliers

UK

Consult the telephone directory for details of your local garden centre or timber merchant.

Timber and decking

Andrew's Timber
387 Blackfen Road
Blackfen, Sidcup
Kent DA13 9NJ
Tel/fax: 020 8303 2696
www.andrews-timber.co.uk
(Timber, decking,
accessories)

Sandalwood Gates
     & Timber Products
Elvington Industrial
     Estate
York Road
Elvington, York
YO4 5AR
Tel/fax: 01904 608542
www.sandalwoodgates.co.uk
(Fencing, timberwork
and decking products)

Travis Perkins
     Trading Co. Ltd
Head Office:
Lodge Way House
Lodge Way
Harlestone Road
Northampton
NN5 7UG
Tel: 01604 752424
www.travisperkins.co.uk
(Builders' merchants
supplying timber and
decking products;
branches nationwide)

Tool manufacturers

Black & Decker
210 Bath Road
Slough, Berkshire
SL1 3YD
Tel: 01753 567 055

Stanley UK Ltd
The Stanley Works
Woodside, Sheffield
Yorkshire S3 9PD
Tel: 0114 276 8888

Tool retailers

Industrial Tool Supplies
     (London) Ltd
607–617 High Road
     Leyton
London E10 6RF
Tel: 020 8539 2231
www.itslondon.co.uk

S J Carter Tools Ltd
Gloucester House
10 Camberwell
     New Road
London SE5 0TA
Tel: 020 7587 1222

General DIY stores (outlets nationwide)

B & Q plc
Head Office:
Portswood House
1 Hampshire
     Corporate Park
Chandlers Ford
Eastleigh, Hampshire
SO53 3YX
Tel: 01703 256256

Focus Do-It-All
     Group Ltd
Head Office:
Gawsworth House
Westmere Drive
Crewe
Cheshire CW1 6XB
Tel: 01384 456456

Homebase Ltd
Beddington House
Railway Approach
Wallington
Surrey
SM6 0HB
Tel: 020 8784 7200

Wickes
Wickes House
120–138 Station Road
Harrow, Middlesex
HA1 2QB
Tel: 0870 6089001
www.wickes.co.uk

AUSTRALIA

General DIY stores

ABC Timbers and
     Building Supplies
46 Auburn Road
Regents Park
NSW 2143
Tel: 02 9645 2511
(Tools, fittings, fixtures
and a complete range
of hardware)

BBC Hardware and
     Hardwarehouse
     (Head Office)
Building A
Corner Cambridge &
     Chester Streets
Epping, NSW 2121
Tel: 02 9876 0888
www.bbchardware.com.au
www.hardwarehouse.com.au

Bowens Timber and
     Building Supplies
48 Hallam Road South
Hallam, VIC 3803
Tel: 03 9796 3003
www.bowens.com.au
(Timber, tools
and hardware)

Mitre 10 Australia Ltd
     (Head Office)
122 Newton Road
Wetherill Park
NSW 2164
Tel: 02 9725 3222
www.mitre10.com.au
Customer Services:
1800 777 850

NEW ZEALAND

General DIY stores

Mitre 10
Head Office:
182 Wairau Road
Glenfield, Auckland
Tel: 09 443 9900
(Branches nationwide)

Placemakers
     Support Office
150 Marua Road
Private Bag 14942
Panmure, Auckland
Tel: 09 525 5100

Timber

Rosenfeld Kidson
513 Mount Wellington
     Highway
Mount Wellington
Auckland
Tel: 09 573 0503

South Pacific Timber
Corner Ruru &
     Shaddock Streets
Auckland City
Tel: 09 379 5150

Timpan City Ltd
21 Walls Road
Penrose, Auckland
Tel: 09 571 0020

Wilson Bros Timber
71 Foremans Road
Hornby
Tel: 03 688 2336

SOUTH AFRICA

Tool retailers

Bluff Mica Hardware &
     Building Supplies
28 Lighthouse Road
Durban 4052
Tel: 031 466 1068

Jack's Paint &
     Hardware
221 Louis Botha Ave
Johannesburg 2192
Tel: 011 640 5067

Mica Hardware
198 Lansdowne Road
Claremont
Cape Town 7700
Tel: 021 683 7821

Wardkiss Paint and
     Hardware Centre
329 Sydney Road
Durban 4001
Tel: 031 205 1551

Worcester Mica
     Hardware
Corner Tulbach &
     Baring Street
Worcester 6850
Tel: 023 347 0477

Timber

Citiwood
339 Main Reef Road
Denver
Johannesburg 2094
Tel: 011 622 9360
     (ext. 10)

Coleman Timbers
Unit 3, Willowfield
     Crescent
Springfield Park
Durban 4091
Tel: 031 579 1565

Lumber City
6 Marconi Road
Montague Gardens
Cape Town 7441
Tel: 021 551 2635

Penny Pinchers
351 Lansdowne Road
Lansdowne
Cape Town 7780
Tel: 021 696 2990

Index

AG&G Books would like to thank Garden and Wildlife Matters Photographic Library for contributing the photographs used on pages 6, 7 and 18-23.